In His Own Words

THE TESTIMONY OF JESUS REGARDING HIMSELF

JOHN K. LASHELL

Cover design by
Logan Hall

ISBN: 9798683221638

DEDICATION

To those who have been shaken by the challenge: Jesus never claimed he was divine.

CONTENTS

Why This Book?

— ❧ —

"**J**esus never said He was the Son of God," claimed my professor. It was the winter of 1966, and I was a freshman at the University of California, San Diego. I didn't know any better at the time. Neither did the young lady in our church who heard exactly the same claim a few years ago in her college religion class.

However, Jesus clearly identified Himself as the Son of God in John 5:17-30, and He acknowledged that He had said, "I am the Son of God" in John 10:36. Moreover, when Simon Peter said, "You are the Christ, the Son of the living God," Jesus replied, "Blessed are you Simon Barjona, because flesh and blood did not reveal this to you, but my Father who is in heaven" (Matthew 16:16-17). At His Jewish trial, when the high priest asked Jesus, "Are you the Christ, the Son of the blessed One?" the Lord answered, "I am" (Mark 14:61-62).

Even more outrageous is the notion, popularized by Dan Brown, that Jesus was not regarded as divine until the Council of Nicea in AD 325. The truth is that both orthodox Christians and those deemed heretics taught the divinity of Jesus. Even the Gnostics, whom Brown claims to have read, regarded Jesus as divine. The issue at Nicea was the *precise sense* in which Jesus is divine. Only the invincibly ignorant will say about such a well-documented historical fact, "Well, that's just your opinion." That popular retort—I've heard it—is a fool's way of protecting his own ignorance.

Then there are the cultists who go two by two throughout your neighborhood. They claim that the Bible does not teach the doctrine of the Trinity. It is true, of course, that the word Trinity never occurs in the Bible. However, the truths summarized by *Trinity* are clearly taught throughout the Scriptures.± Perhaps you have attempted to show the visitors at your door John 1:1, which says, "the Word [Christ] was God." If you did, they certainly trotted out their corrupt translation, which says, "the word was a god."

At this point, many Christians do not know what to say. Probably neither they, nor the cultists know Greek, so all each side can do is repeat, "My Bible says…" When cult members go on to insist that Jesus cannot be God because He said, "My Father is greater than I" (John 14:28), all the average believer can do is to shut the door in their faces. I deal briefly with the cultists and the Gnostics in the last two chapters, but for now I want to introduce the primary focus of this book.

± See chapter 11 for a brief summary of the doctrine of the Trinity.

Our belief in the deity of Christ does not depend on two or three well-known verses. Jesus constantly said things that would be blasphemous on the lips of anyone but God. You may have read C. S. Lewis's famous trilemma about Christ. After referring to some of the outrageous claims of Jesus, he concluded,

> I am trying here to prevent anyone saying the really foolish thing that people often say about Him: I'm ready to accept Jesus as a great moral teacher, but I don't accept his claim to be God. That is the one thing we must not say. A man who was merely a man and said the sort of things Jesus said would not be a great moral teacher. He would either be a lunatic — on the level with the man who says he is a poached egg — or else he would be the Devil of Hell. You must make your choice. Either this man was, and is, the Son of God, or else a madman or something worse. You can shut him up for a fool, you can spit at him and kill him as a demon or you can fall at his feet and call him Lord and God, but let us not come with any patronizing nonsense about his being a great human teacher. He has not left that open to us. He did not intend to (Lewis 40-41).

My goal in the following pages is to compare the claims of Christ with what the Old Testament teaches us about the one, true, and living God. On page after page of the gospels, Jesus applies to Himself privileges and titles that only God can claim. Since the synoptic gospels (Matthew, Mark, and Luke) frequently receive less emphasis in discussions of Christ's deity than the gospel of John does, I will initially focus more attention on their testimony before turning to the fourth gospel.

Chapter 1

Jesus and the Prophets

— ❦ —

Cultural Christians, and most other despisers of the biblical Jesus, approve of the Sermon on the Mount. After all, it contains their favorite verse, "Do not judge so that you will not be judged" (Matthew 7:1). Of course, they fail to notice that later in the same chapter, Jesus tells us how to judge false prophets. Never mind that. Isn't the essential message of the Sermon on the Mount, "Be nice to everybody, and they will be nice to you?"

Well, in a word, NO! The Sermon on the Mount tells us how to live a life of radical discipleship as citizens of the kingdom of heaven. And who is the king of that kingdom? It is Jesus. Consider what He says about Himself in the opening paragraph of the sermon:

> Blessed are those who have been persecuted for the sake of righteousness, for theirs is the kingdom of heaven. Blessed are you when people insult you and persecute you, and falsely say all kinds of evil against you because of Me. Rejoice and be glad, for your reward in heaven is great; for in the same way they persecuted the prophets who were before you (Matthew 5:10-12).

Look carefully at what Jesus is saying. Persecution for the sake of righteousness is not persecution for being a nice, law-abiding citizen. It is equivalent to persecution for the sake of Jesus. Furthermore, the disciples of Jesus are like the prophets of old who were persecuted for delivering the message of Yahweh. The prophets were hated for God's sake. The disciples are hated for Jesus' sake. This parallel is strengthened in subsequent sayings of Jesus.

Jesus Sends Prophets

Near the end of His earthly ministry, Jesus said to the Pharisees who had rejected Him,

> Therefore, behold, I am sending you prophets and wise men and scribes; some of them you will kill and crucify, and some of them you will scourge in your synagogues, and persecute from city to city, so that upon you may fall the guilt of all the righteous blood shed on earth, from the blood of righteous Abel to the blood of Zechariah, the son of Berechiah, whom you murdered between the temple and the altar.... Jerusalem, Jerusalem, who kills the prophets and stones those who are sent to her (Matthew 23: 34-35, 37a)!

The whole Old Testament clearly teaches that neither angels nor great men send the prophets. God, and God alone, has that prerogative. Yet Jesus says He will send prophets. Compare His words with the following quotations.

To the rebellious Jews of Jeremiah's day, Yahweh± said, "Since the day that your fathers came out of the

---

± *Yahweh* is the most likely pronunciation of the Old

land of Egypt until this day, I have sent you all My servants the prophets, daily rising early and sending them" (Jeremiah 7:25-26). "Listen to the words of My servants the prophets, whom I have been sending to you again and again, but you have not listened" (Jeremiah 26:5). "Also I have sent to you all My servants the prophets, sending them again and again" (Jeremiah 35:15).

God was patient and persistent. He did not send Israel one messenger. He sent them many prophets throughout their long, rebellious history. Likewise, Jesus predicted that He would be sending "prophets and wise men and scribes" who would encounter determined, implacable rejection. Moreover, Jesus places His prophetic messengers on the same plane as the prophets of old who warned to rebellious Jerusalem.

Under His Wings

Earlier in this chapter I quoted only the first part of Matthew 23:37. Here is the whole of it.

> Jerusalem, Jerusalem, who kills the prophets and stones those who are sent to her! How often I wanted to gather your children together, the way a hen gathers her chicks under her wings, and you were unwilling.

Testament name for God. (*Jehovah* is more familiar, but it is based on a misunderstanding of the Hebrew vowel points.) This name occurs over 6,000 times in the Hebrew Old Testament and never in the Greek New Testament. Most English translations of the Old Testament represent *Yahweh* by LORD or GOD, in small capitals.

Here, Jesus claims that He is the One who sent the Old Testament prophets in an effort to gather the "children" of Jerusalem under His wings. (In biblical terminology, the children of a city are its inhabitants.)

To come under the wings of Yahweh is to find refuge and protection in Him. For example, Boaz blessed the foreigner Ruth because she had left her father's house and her father's gods, saying "May the LORD reward your work, and your wages be full from the LORD, the God of Israel, under whose wings you have come to seek refuge" (Ruth 2:12). When David fled from Saul, he prayed, "My soul takes refuge in You; and in the shadow of Your wings I will take refuge until destruction passes by" (Psalm 57:1). Similar expressions occur in Psalm 17:8; 36:7; and 91:4.

Jesus did not simply *invite* the Old Testament Jewish people to take shelter under His wings. Hundreds of years before He was born on earth, He actively sought to *gather* them under His wings. He said, "How often I wanted to gather your children." Gathering His people is another work of God. What Yahweh sought to do through His prophets, He will effectively do when He gathers the dispersed refugees of Israel at the end of the age:

> If your outcasts are at the ends of the earth, from there the LORD your God will gather you, and from there He will bring you back (Deuteronomy 30:4).

> For a brief moment I forsook you,
> But with great compassion I will gather you
> (Isaiah 54:7).

Similar expressions are common throughout the Old Testament.

Prophets and angels do not gather the people of God to themselves, but Jesus uses prophets and preachers to seek and to gather His lost ones under His wings to protect them from the wrath to come.

When I was a child, one of the stories that fascinated me was the colorfully illustrated parable of *The Little Red Hen* by Mrs. Floyd McCague. One day a mother hen sensed the danger of a rapidly approaching prairie fire. She clucked to her little chicks to come and find shelter under her wings. After the fire had swept through the barnyard, the farmer returned. There he found the charred body of the little red hen, but when he pushed her over with his foot, her little chicks scurried out from under her blackened wings. One little chick, however, had refused to listen to his mother's call, and he was found burned and dead a few feet away from her. The lesson to my childish heart was clear. Listen to the call of Jesus. He is seeking to gather His little ones to protect them from the coming fire of judgment.

Hated for Jesus' Sake

In the sermon on the Mount, Jesus said that His disciples would be hated *for His sake*. This is a common theme in the teaching of Jesus.

> Brother will betray brother to death, and a father his child; and children will rise up against parents and cause them to be put to death. You will be hated by all because of My name, but it is the one who has endured to the end

who will be saved (Matthew 10:21-22).

Then they will deliver you to tribulation, and will kill you, and you will be hated by all nations because of My name (Matthew 24:9).

Remember the word that I said to you, "A slave is not greater than his master." If they persecuted Me, they will also persecute you; if they kept My word, they will keep yours also. But all these things they will do to you for My name's sake, because they do not know the One who sent Me (John 15:20).

In 2018 David S. Buckel, a nationally known attorney, burned himself alive as a protest against the widespread use of fossil fuels. The Bible never encourages people to commit suicide for some cause that is dear to them. That idea is entirely foreign to the biblical way of thinking and speaking. God's people, however, frequently suffer for the sake of the Lord. They suffer for their allegiance to *Him*, not to a cause:

> For Your sake we are killed all day long;
> We are considered as sheep to be slaughtered
> (Psalm 44:22).

> Because for Your sake I have borne reproach;
> Dishonor has covered my face.
> I have become estranged from my brothers
> And an alien to my mother's sons.
> For zeal for Your house has consumed me,
> And the reproaches of those who reproach You have
> fallen on me (Psalm 69:7-9).

> You who know, O LORD,
> Remember me, take notice of me,
> And take vengeance for me on my persecutors.
> Do not, in view of Your patience, take me away;
> Know that for Your sake I endure reproach
> (Jeremiah 15:15).

The disciples and prophets of Jesus suffer for His sake just as godly prophets of old suffered for speaking in the name of Yahweh. No angel, or no mere man, has the authority to command us to suffer for his sake, but Jesus does.

Before He was born, Jesus sent the prophets of the Old Covenant to preach to Israel and to suffer. (Don't miss the astounding boldness of this claim!) Under the New Covenant, He sent first-century prophets, and He continues to send "wise men and scribes" to suffer in His name (Matthew 23:34). He has the right to do this because He is God.

He has the right to command you and me to speak in His name and to suffer for His sake because He is God. Will you speak boldly and yet gently in the name of Christ even in the face of ridicule—or worse? Are you willing to be sent by Him into your workplace, your neighborhood, or around the world, no matter what the outcome may be?

Chapter 2

Jesus and Our Families

— ✆ —

The congregation of my first church in rural Wisconsin was so small that I could easily have visited every family once a week. Instead, I went door to door seeking new people. One evening, I ended up in the living room of a family that was watching a Billy Graham crusade on television. When the program was over, I said, "If you had been there, would you have gone forward to receive Christ?"

They answered, "Probably."

I said, "Would you like to receive Him now?"

They said they would, and they did—all of them. Not long afterwards, I baptized them, and they became regular attenders at the church. Unfortunately, conversion did not immediately transform an unhappy family into a joyous one. On more than one occasion, the lady of the house came to me with an unusual request.

She would begin by pointing out passages such as the following:

> If anyone comes to Me, and does not hate his own father and mother and wife and children and brothers and

sisters, yes, and even his own life, he cannot be My
disciple (Luke 14:26).

And He said to them, "Truly I say to you, there is no one
who has left house or wife or brothers or parents or
children, for the sake of the kingdom of God, who will
not receive many times as much at this time and in the
age to come, eternal life" (Luke 18:29-30).

Then she would beg me to send her as a missionary to
another country. Perhaps some of the Lord's precepts
seemed rather burdensome, but not this one. She thought
it would be a relief to leave her family for Jesus' sake. I
kid you not. This actually happened.

Though this lady was misguided, her notions were
close to actual the experiences of many missionaries.
Today's tearful goodbyes at the airport are little in
comparison with what nineteenth-century servants of
Christ considered routine.

John Paton, missionary to the New Hebrides (now
Vanuatu), buried his first wife and infant son on an
island filled with cannibals. (He slept for some time on
their graves to prevent the natives from exhuming and
devouring them.) Not long afterwards, he barely escaped
with his own life. A few years later, he returned to a
neighboring island with his second wife. Though the
majority of the indigenous population on this island were
eventually converted, the Patons were frequently in
danger of losing their lives. They also had to endure
year-long separations from their school-age children. For
them, as for many missionaries, the calling of Christ
meant putting Him above their families.

Family Loyalty in the Old Testament

To put in perspective Jesus' insistence that we love Him more than we love our families, we need to go back to the Old Testament. I begin with the respect children are supposed to have for their parents.

> Honor your father and your mother, that your days may be prolonged in the land which the LORD your God gives you (Exodus 20:12).

> He who curses his father or his mother shall surely be put to death (Exodus 21:17).

Jesus quoted both of these passages in Matthew 15:4 to highlight the respect and care children should have for their parents. Lack of such respect was so serious that it is scathingly denounced in the Old Testament. For example,

> The eye that mocks a father
> And scorns a mother,
> The ravens of the valley will pick it out,
> And the young eagles will eat it (Proverbs 30:17).

On the other hand, parents properly love and care for their offspring: "A good man leaves an inheritance to his children's children" (Proverbs 13:22). A mother's love is so natural and good that we are shocked when a mother murders her child. God's love is like a mother's love, only better:

> Can a woman forget her nursing child
> And have no compassion on the son of her womb?
> Even these may forget, but I will not forget you (Isaiah 49:15).

What is important enough to warrant breaking the bonds of familial duty and affection? Loyalty to God supersedes loyalty to family.

> If your brother, your mother's son, or your son or daughter, or the wife you cherish, or your friend who is as your own soul, entice you secretly, saying, "Let us go and serve other gods" (whom neither you nor your fathers have known, of the gods of the peoples who are around you, near you or far from you, from one end of the earth to the other end), you shall not yield to him or listen to him; and your eye shall not pity him, nor shall you spare or conceal him. But you shall surely kill him; your hand shall be first against him to put him to death, and afterwards the hand of all the people. So you shall stone him to death because he has sought to seduce you from the LORD your God who brought you out from the land of Egypt, out of the house of slavery (Deuteronomy 13:6-10).

I hasten to add that we are no longer under this provision of the Mosaic Law. That harsh sentence was part of God's zealous determination to preserve true faith in Israel until Christ came. However, it is clear that loyalty to God trumps loyalty to family.

Loving Family More Than God

I heard recently about a man who gave a Bible to his unbelieving sister. The next day she died in a car accident. This man became bitter and has backed away from church or any discussion of spiritual things. His love for his sister was apparently greater than his love for God. Probably most of us have loved ones who will spend eternity in hell. Oh, how that thought pains us! It torments us. But the question we must face is *who holds first place in our hearts?*

It is an old, old temptation, for Adam loved his wife more than he loved God, so he followed her into sin and death. Men are supposed to love their wives with a self-sacrificing love as Christ loved the church (Ephesians 5:25), but sin enters when a man loves his wife more than he loves God.

I have often seen children pull their families out of church after the parents have pushed those children into sports. Team sports on Sunday capture the child's heart. The father's heart has already been captured by Sunday afternoon football, so he has no moral authority to keep his child from playing on Sunday. The parents love the child's present happiness more than they love the child's eternal wellbeing and more than they love God. The result? Church attendance becomes an occasional event (in between games and practice sessions), and ten years later the parents bewail their child's lack of faith.

Even without that kind of parental short-sightedness, families are divided. Apart from the gracious work of the Holy Spirit opening our eyes, we are blind to Christ and hostile to God. As the prophet Micah put it,

> For son treats father contemptuously,
> Daughter rises up against her mother,
> Daughter-in-law against her mother-in-law;
> A man's enemies are the men of his own household
> (Micah 7:6).

Wait, doesn't that sound like something Jesus said? Yes, indeed:

> Do not think that I came to bring peace on the earth; I did not come to bring peace, but a sword. For I came to set a man against his father, and a daughter against her mother, and a daughter-in-law against her mother-in-law; and a man's enemies will be the members of his household. He who loves father or mother more than Me is not worthy of Me; and he who loves son or daughter more than Me is not worthy of Me (Matthew 10:34-37).

It is not just an accident or poor family dynamics that creates a spiritual division between two people who would naturally love each other. Jesus divides people. He slices down through those natural ties and demands whole-hearted devotion for Himself.

Jesus was not asking any more or any less for Himself than the Lord God required of Old Testament believers. God told Jeremiah not to marry and raise sons and daughters (Jeremiah 16:2). In order to be God's prophet, he had to set aside his natural human desire for a family. Here's another example: One morning God told Ezekiel that his wife would die, and the prophecy came to pass that very evening. She was "the desire of [his] eyes," but the Lord would not permit him to weep or mourn for her (Ezekiel 24:16). God used her death and the hiding of Ezekiel's grief as a prophetic parable for the people. Wow! That was harsh. It was *a severe mercy*.±

± *A Severe Mercy* is the title of a great book by Sheldon Vanauken, who also lost his beloved wife. The title comes

Does the demand of Jesus—that you put Him first in your life above your family—does this demand shock you? It should. Would it have shocked a first-century Jew? Absolutely! He would have understood that no one but the Lord God has the right to demand such allegiance.

> Hear, O Israel! The LORD is our God, the LORD is one! You shall love the LORD your God with all your heart and with all your soul and with all your might (Deuteronomy 6:4-5).

If Jesus was not God, He was setting Himself up as a deliberate rival to God. So, He was either God or a demon from hell. You choose.

Think about whether there are family ties that threaten to pull you away from Christ and His church. If the devil discovers that a family picnic or a birthday party for Aunt Matilda's dog is enough to keep you out of church, you won't be worshiping with other believers three Sundays out of four. Do you resent God because a loved one has died in unbelief and is now suffering the wrath of God? Has God called you to a ministry that would move you away from your family, and are you hesitating to go because you love them so much? Does your faith in Christ create so much friction with your relatives that you are beginning to think following Jesus is just not worth it?

Jesus is worth it. Jesus is more important than your father, your mother, your sister or brother. Jesus is more

---

from Augustine's *Confessions* (8.11).

important than your wife or husband or children. Jesus all by Himself will be enough for you because He is God, but since He loves you, He will give you even more.

> Jesus said, "Truly I say to you, there is no one who has left house or brothers or sisters or mother or father or children or farms, for My sake and for the gospel's sake, but that he will receive a hundred times as much now in the present age, houses and brothers and sisters and mothers and children and farms, along with persecutions; and in the age to come, eternal life" (Mark 10:29-30).

The church will be your family when your family turns its back on you. "If my father and my mother forsake me, then the Lord will take me up" (Psalm 27:10, marginal reading).

Chapter 3

Jesus and Judgment

"**J**esus is cool. He's my good buddy. He's really into love and happiness. He wants me happy. He wants you to be happy. He wants everybody to be happy. So, go do your own thing and as long as you don't hurt nobody, He'll be good with that."

Really? The Bible says that God created man in His own image, and some wit has remarked that man has often returned the compliment. Refashioning Jesus into our own image has become almost a cottage industry these days, and Jesus, "my good buddy," is probably not the worst example.

Jesus the Judge

Let's go back to the Sermon on the Mount. You know the one—it's Jesus' message about being nice to everybody and condemning nobody: "Do unto others as you would have them do unto you," and all that. Near the end of the sermon, Jesus said,

> Not everyone who says to Me, "Lord, Lord," will enter the kingdom of heaven, but he who does the will of My Father who is in heaven will enter. Many will say to Me on that day, "Lord, Lord, did we not prophesy in Your name, and in Your name cast out demons, and in Your

name perform many miracles?" And then I will declare to them, "I never knew you; depart from Me, you who practice lawlessness" (Matthew 7:21-23).

Notice first that Jesus claims to be the one who will either let people into the kingdom of heaven or expel them from the kingdom. He will not listen to the pious professions of religious shysters. He will examine their deeds and convict them of breaking the law of God.

Second, notice three things this saying implies: Jesus has the authority to judge; *and* He has the knowledge of each man's deeds so that His judgment is just; *and* He has the power to enforce His judgments. There is no appeal and no escape from His judgment.

The classic New Testament parable on judgment is found in Matthew 25:

> But when the Son of Man comes in His glory, and all the angels with Him, then He will sit on His glorious throne. All the nations will be gathered before Him; and He will separate them from one another, as the shepherd separates the sheep from the goats; and He will put the sheep on His right, and the goats on the left (vv. 31-33).

To those whose lives indicate true conversion, "the King will say to those on His right, 'Come, you who are blessed of My Father, inherit the kingdom prepared for you from the foundation of the world'" (v. 34). The rest will hear these scorching words from the lips of gentle Jesus, meek and mild, "Depart from Me, accursed ones, into the eternal fire which has been prepared for the devil and his angels" (v. 41).

The imagery of separating sheep and goats comes from the Old Testament:

> As for you, My flock, thus says the Lord GOD, "Behold, I will judge between one sheep and another, between the rams and the male goats."

> Therefore, thus says the Lord GOD to them, "Behold, I, even I, will judge between the fat sheep and the lean sheep. Because you push with side and with shoulder, and thrust at all the weak with your horns until you have scattered them abroad, therefore, I will deliver My flock, and they will no longer be a prey; and I will judge between one sheep and another" (Ezekiel 34:17, 20-22).

As the Lord Yahweh judged His flock Israel in the Old Testament, so Jesus will judge the sheep and the goats of all the nations when He comes in His glory.

Jesus Forgave Sins

On at least two occasions Jesus, the judge, asserted His right to render a verdict of acquittal as He forgave sins in His own name and on His own authority. To a paralyzed man Jesus said,

> "Friend, your sins are forgiven you." The scribes and the Pharisees began to reason, saying, "Who is this man who speaks blasphemies? Who can forgive sins, but God alone?" But Jesus, aware of their reasonings, answered and said to them, "Why are you reasoning in your hearts? Which is easier, to say, 'Your sins have been forgiven you,' or to say, 'Get up and walk'? But, so that you may know that the Son of Man has authority on earth to forgive sins,"—He said to the paralytic—"I say to you, get up, and pick up your stretcher and go home" (Luke 5:20-24).

While dining at the house of a certain Pharisee, Jesus forgave a notoriously immoral woman.

> Then He said to her, "Your sins have been forgiven." Those who were reclining at the table with Him began to say to themselves, "Who is this man who even forgives sins?" And He said to the woman, "Your faith has saved you; go in peace" (Luke 7:48-50).

The Pharisees were quite properly shocked when Jesus forgave sinners. They knew from the Old Testament that no prophet had ever dared to forgive someone on his own authority. The closest parallel to Jesus' declaration of pardon comes from the lips of Nathan the prophet. After David committed adultery with Bathsheba and arranged for her husband to be killed, he spent a miserable year overwhelmed with remorse and guilt. (See Psalm 32:3-4.) Finally, Nathan confronted him, and David repented: "Then David said to Nathan, 'I have sinned against the LORD.' And Nathan said to David, 'The LORD also has taken away your sin; you shall not die'" (2 Samuel 12:13).

The difference between Nathan and Jesus is striking. Nathan the prophet announced what God had revealed to him—that the Lord had forgiven David. If Jesus had said to the paralytic, "The Lord has forgiven you," He would have placed Himself on the same level as an Old Testament prophet. Jesus, however, declared in the most absolute terms that He had the authority to forgive sins.

Old Testament saints appealed to the Lord, not to the prophets for the forgiveness of sins:

> For Your name's sake, O LORD,
> Pardon my iniquity for it is great (Psalm 25:11).

Yahweh, the LORD, says,

> I, even I, am the one who wipes out your
>   transgressions for My own sake,
> And I will not remember your sins (Isaiah 43:25).

So, Micah summarizes and celebrates the difference between Yahweh and all other gods:

> Who is a God like You, who pardons iniquity
> And passes over the rebellious act of the remnant of
>   His possession?
> He does not retain His anger forever,
> Because He delights in unchanging love
> (Micah 7:18).

There is no god like Yahweh who pardons sin and who wipes out transgressions. If Jesus is not Yahweh, He is Yahweh's boldest rival.

Honor the Father and the Son

God reserves to Himself the right of judging sinners. He does not share this ultimate authority with any merely human being:

> Say among the nations, "The LORD reigns;
> Indeed, the world is firmly established, it will not
>   be moved;
> He will judge the peoples with equity (Psalm 96:10).

> A jealous and avenging God is the LORD;
> The LORD is avenging and wrathful.
> The LORD takes vengeance on His adversaries,
> And He reserves wrath for His enemies.
> The LORD is slow to anger and great in power,
> And the LORD will by no means leave the guilty
>   unpunished.

> In whirlwind and storm is His way,
> And clouds are the dust beneath His feet....
> Who can stand before His indignation?
> Who can endure the burning of His anger?
> His wrath is poured out like fire
> And the rocks are broken up by Him
> (Nahum 1:2-3, 6).

> Vengeance is Mine, and retribution,
> In due time their foot will slip;
> For the day of their calamity is near,
> And the impending things are hastening upon
>   them (Deuteronomy 32:35).

We have seen in Matthew and Luke that Jesus claims for Himself the right to forgive and to condemn. He is the Judge of all men. In John 5, He asserts this right in the most forcible terms:

> For not even the Father judges anyone, but He has given all judgment to the Son, so that all will honor the Son even as they honor the Father. He who does not honor the Son does not honor the Father who sent Him. Truly, truly, I say to you, he who hears My word, and believes Him who sent Me, has eternal life, and does not come into judgment, but has passed out of death into life. Truly, truly, I say to you, an hour is coming and now is, when the dead will hear the voice of the Son of God, and those who hear will live. For just as the Father has life in Himself, even so He gave to the Son also to have life in Himself; and He gave Him authority to execute judgment, because He is the Son of Man. Do not marvel at this; for an hour is coming, in which all who are in the tombs will hear His voice, and will come forth; those who did the good deeds to a resurrection of life, those who committed the evil deeds to a resurrection of judgment (vv. 22-29).

Jesus is fit to judge all men because He is the Son of God *and* the Son of Man. As the Son of God, He speaks with divine authority. As the Son of Man, He judges with human insight and compassion.

One other aspect of this passage deserves close attention. God the Father wants all people to honor His Son just as they honor Him. This is striking because the Lord cannot, He will not, share His honor with any created being.

> I am the LORD, that is My name;
> I will not give My glory to another,
> Nor My praise to graven images. (Isaiah 42:8).

> For My own sake, for My own sake, I will act;
> For how can My name be profaned?
> And My glory I will not give to another
> (Isaiah 48:11).

For God to share His divine honor and glory with any created being would be for Him to lie about His own intrinsic worth. Do you see the astounding thing that Jesus was claiming? Jesus said that all men should honor Him in the same way that they are obligated to honor the Father. Do you see why the Jews wanted to kill Him?

Jesus said that He will be the final judge of all people. There will be no court of appeals above Him. What, therefore, will be His verdict in your case? Will you be acquitted, not because you are good enough in yourself, but because you have cast yourself on the mercy of the court and been forgiven? Will you try to bluff your way into heaven by claiming that your good deeds outweigh the bad? Jesus will look right through you and see the hollowness of your boast. Will Jesus, the judge of all flesh, be your Savior or your executioner?

Chapter 4

Jesus Gives Rest

— ✍ —

In his famous *Confessions,* St. Augustine said, "Thou hast formed us for Thyself, and our hearts are restless till they find rest in Thee" (1.1). We are troubled by outward trials and by inward turmoil until Jesus gives us His peace. According to the gospels, the peace of Christ is none other than the peace of God.

God Stills the Storms

God commanded Jonah to go and preach to Nineveh. This was highly displeasing to the prophet because Nineveh was a royal city of Israel's fierce enemy, Assyria. Jonah was afraid that Nineveh would repent and thus escape God's judgment for a time. (That is exactly what happened.)

When Jonah boarded a ship to flee from the presence of the Lord and to escape his prophetic responsibility, "The LORD hurled a great wind on the sea and there was a great storm on the sea so that the ship was about to break up" (Jonah 1:4).
The frightened sailors drew lots to see on whose account this fearful storm had come. The lot fell on Jonah, who

27

confessed his rebellion against Yahweh. When he told the sailors to cast him overboard, they initially refused, but finally they yielded.

> Then they called on the LORD and said, "We earnestly pray, O LORD, do not let us perish on account of this man's life and do not put innocent blood on us; for You, O LORD, have done as You have pleased." So they picked up Jonah, threw him into the sea, and the sea stopped its raging. Then the men feared the LORD greatly, and they offered a sacrifice to the LORD and made vows (Jonah 1:14-16).

This may be the only occasion in history when tossing a man overboard resulted in several conversions. It's probably not a good evangelistic strategy for our imitation.

Jonah did not still the storm. Yahweh did, so the men feared Yahweh and offered a sacrifice to Him. Throughout the Old Testament God is the one who raises storms and who stills them.

> O LORD God of hosts,
> Who is like You, O mighty LORD?
> Your faithfulness also surrounds You.
> You rule the swelling of the sea;
> When its waves rise, You still them (Psalm 89:8-9).

> Those who go down to the sea in ships,
> Who do business on great waters;
> They have seen the works of the LORD,
> And His wonders in the deep.
> For He spoke and raised up a stormy wind,
> Which lifted up the waves of the sea.
> They rose up to the heavens, they went down to
>   the depths;
> Their soul melted away in their misery.

> They reeled and staggered like a drunken man,
> And were at their wits' end.
> Then they cried to the LORD in their trouble,
> And He brought them out of their distresses.
> He caused the storm to be still,
> So that the waves of the sea were hushed
> (Psalm 107:23-29).

Notice now the parallels between these passages and the account of Jesus stilling a storm on the Sea of Galilee:

> On that day, when evening came, He said to them, "Let us go over to the other side." Leaving the crowd, they took Him along with them in the boat, just as He was; and other boats were with Him. And there arose a fierce gale of wind, and the waves were breaking over the boat so much that the boat was already filling up. Jesus Himself was in the stern, asleep on the cushion; and they woke Him and said to Him, "Teacher, do You not care that we are perishing?" And He got up and rebuked the wind and said to the sea, "Hush, be still." And the wind died down and it became perfectly calm. And He said to them, "Why are you afraid? Do you still have no faith?" They became very much afraid and said to one another, "Who then is this, that even the wind and the sea obey Him?" (Mark 4:35-41).

As in Psalm 107 and Jonah 1, the storm was so fierce that the boat was in danger of sinking. Like the sailors in Jonah, the disciples feared Him who stilled the storm more than they feared the wind and the waves. The stilling of the storm by Jesus was more than a nature miracle. The narrative parallels Him to the storm-stilling God of the Old Testament. Jesus did not say to the waves and the wind, "The Lord rebuke you," as an Old

Testament prophet might have done. He rebuked the elements on His own authority.

Jesus Gives Rest

In the gospels, Jesus gives rest and peace to troubled souls, just as He stills the troubled sea:

> Come to Me, all who are weary and heavy-laden, and I will give you rest. Take My yoke upon you and learn from Me, for I am gentle and humble in heart, and you will find rest for your souls. For My yoke is easy and My burden is light (Matthew 11:28-30).

Rest of soul! How desirable and yet how difficult to obtain! Apart from Jesus we can find nothing better than a superficial rest, a rest that ignores the underlying restlessness of sin.

> But the wicked are like the tossing sea,
> For it cannot be quiet,
> And its waters toss up refuse and mud.
> "There is no peace," says my God, "for the wicked"
> (Isaiah 57:20-21).

What is the source of true rest and peace? In the Old Testament it is clearly Yahweh.

> "I have seen his ways, but I will heal him;
> I will lead him and restore comfort to him and to
>   his mourners,
> Creating the praise of the lips.
> Peace, peace to him who is far and to him who is
>   near,"
> Says the LORD, "and I will heal him"
> (Isaiah 57:18-19).

> And He said, "My presence shall go with you, and I will give you rest" (Exodus 33:14).

Thus says the LORD,
"Stand by the ways and see and ask for the ancient
      paths,
Where the good way is, and walk in it;
And you will find rest for your souls.
But they said, 'We will not walk in it'"
(Jeremiah 6:16).

When Jesus used the phrase, "you will find rest for your souls," He was clearly quoting from Jeremiah, and He was claiming that He could give the rest that Yahweh had promised. His promises of peace are no less striking.

> Peace I leave with you; My peace I give to you; not as the world gives do I give to you. Do not let your heart be troubled, nor let it be fearful (John 14:27).

> These things I have spoken to you, so that in Me you may have peace. In the world you have tribulation, but take courage; I have overcome the world (John 16:33).

The peace Jesus gives is His personal peace, and we find it only in union with Him. It is assured because He is victor over all the unsettling forces of the world that attack our souls. The phrase "My peace" is significant because peace is not a commodity that Jesus may give us without giving us Himself. True peace is only in Him.

God accused the false prophets of Jeremiah's day, saying,

> They have healed the brokenness of My people
>   superficially,
> Saying, "Peace, peace,"
> But there is no peace (Jeremiah 6:14).

The Lord, however, offers something much better:

> You keep him in perfect peace whose mind is
>   stayed on you,
> Because he trusts in you (Isaiah 26:3 ESV).

"Perfect peace" is literally *shalōm, shalōm*. The word for peace is repeated, which is the Hebrew equivalent of underlining, italicizing, and capitalizing a word. In the Old Testament, God gives peace. In the New Testament, Jesus gives peace in His own name.

How to Have Peace and Rest

How then can we have the true peace and rest that Jesus offers? Let's return to Matthew 11:28-30.

> Come to Me, all who are weary and heavy-laden, and I will give you rest. Take My yoke upon you and learn from Me, for I am gentle and humble in heart, and you will find rest for your souls. For My yoke is easy and My burden is light.

The way to have Christ's rest is to take His yoke in place of the heavy, wearying burden you are bearing.

Picture in your mind two oxen yoked together with a heavy, wooden bar over their necks. They are attached to a wagon overloaded with immense boulders. The wheels of the wagon are stuck axle-deep in mire while the driver is lacerating the backs of the oxen with a whip tipped with bits of steel. The poor beasts are straining with all their might, but they cannot budge the wagon. That is the plight of suffering men and women laden with their sins and the cares of life, beaten down by the world and the devil.

Now look off to the other side of the road. Another wagon headed the opposite way stands ready with an empty yoke. The driver, Jesus, says, "Come pull My load. It is easy and light." The load looks heavier, if possible than the one the oxen are already attempting to pull. The first large lump on Jesus' wagon is labeled repentance. The second is labeled trust. The third part of the load is labeled obedience to God's will. "Come," says Jesus, "I will not whip you. I will not score your back with lacerations."

One of the poor, beaten beasts bows its head and moans out its acceptance of Jesus as its new master. The Lord takes the blows of the tyrant on His own back as He releases the ox and puts it under His own yoke. As he fastens the lines, He passes His hands across the bleeding back of the animal. The ox lifts its head and lows in gratitude because the sting of the lash has been eased, and its wounds have begun to heal.

Finally, the most amazing thing happens. The Lord Jesus takes on the form of a powerful ox, fits Himself under the other side of the yoke and begins to pull. The great weight of the wagon falls on His shoulders, and his new yoke mate pulls with easy pleasure beside his new master.

When Jesus releases us from slavery to the world, the flesh, and the devil, He doesn't set us loose to wander where we will. He brings us under His yoke. The way to find the rest and peace in Jesus is not to thrash around in the yoke trying to escape it, but rather to submit to it, to lean into it, and to experience the relief that comes when Jesus begins to pull.

Chapter 5

Jesus Is Greater

When I was a student at Moody Bible Institute, I worked on the window-washing crew. We hung out of ten-story windows on straps and climbed tall ladders. Our hazard pay was twenty-five cents an hour more than the rest of the student janitors received.

One of our ladders was a fifty-foot wooden monstrosity that we used to clean the high, arched windows of Torrey Gray Auditorium. Even that was not quite tall enough to reach the peak of the windows unless a fellow was foolish enough to stand on the top rung. We had a couple of guys who would do it; I wasn't one of them.

One day the other guys insisted that I go up the fifty-foot ladder. As I nervously neared the top, one of my co-workers jumped as high as he could and grabbed a rung from the inside. The weight of his body caused the ladder to slide down a foot or so. Then he let go, and the ladder bounced against the wall. I scuttled down, shaken and angry, and I never went up that ladder again.

The top rung of a tall ladder is a precarious place reserved only for the supremely (or foolishly) confident.

In a series of striking claims, Jesus mounted the ladder stretching from earth to heaven until there were no more rungs to climb. Then He stood there, supremely confident in His position and His authority. He calmly claimed to be greater than the greatest men and more holy than Israel's most sacred institutions.

Greater Than the Great Men

More than once the scribes and Pharisees demanded that Jesus show them a sign to support His outrageous claims of authority. What did they want more than feeding five thousand men with a little boy's lunch, or healing the blind, the lame, and the lepers! In the face of such willful blindness, Jesus simply refused.

> But He answered and said to them, "An evil and adulterous generation craves for a sign; and yet no sign will be given to it but the sign of Jonah the prophet; for just as Jonah was three days and three nights in the belly of the sea monster, so will the Son of Man be three days and three nights in the heart of the earth. The men of Nineveh will stand up with this generation at the judgment, and will condemn it because they repented at the preaching of Jonah; and behold, something greater than Jonah is here" (Matthew 12:39-41).

Think for a moment about this claim. We probably count Isaiah, Jeremiah, and Ezekiel as the greatest of the Old Testament prophets, and in terms of the wonderful revelations God gave them, that is certainly true. However, none of them had the kind of response Jonah did. Most of the prophets preached to deaf Israelite ears. Jonah went (under compulsion) to the pagan city of

Nineveh. In Jonah's day Nineveh was one of the royal cities of the Assyrian empire. Later on, it became the capitol. Assyria has a well-deserved reputation as one of the most a ruthless, violent, nations of the ancient world.

One of the Assyrian kings boasts,

> "The monuments which I erect are made of human corpses from which I have cut the head and limbs. I cut off the hands of all those whom I capture alive." Reliefs at Nineveh show men being impaled or flayed, or having their tongues torn out; one shows a king gouging out the eyes of prisoners with a lance while he holds their heads conveniently in place with a cord passed through their lips.

After regaling his readers with these atrocities, Will Durant wryly adds, "As we read such pages we become reconciled to our own mediocrity" (Durant 276).

No wonder Jonah didn't want to preach to them! Nevertheless, he did, and this great city with more than 120,000 morally deficient inhabitants repented. No other Hebrew prophet had such an amazing response to his message—and in this case it was Gentiles who believed.

So in what way was Jesus claiming to be greater than Jonah? First of all, His resurrection from the dead would be a greater miracle than Jonah's preservation in the sea monster. Second, a great pagan city repented at the preaching of Jonah, but an innumerable multitude of Gentiles would be attracted to the message of Jesus. (Matthew 8:11 and 24:31 indicate that Jesus looked forward to gathering many Gentiles into His kingdom.) The Ninevites repented with far less evidence than Jesus provided His contemporaries. He was a far greater prophet than Jonah.

That is the first rung of the ladder. Jesus stands higher than the prophets. The next rung of the ladder places Jesus above the wisest man who ever lived.

> The Queen of the South will rise up with this generation at the judgment and will condemn it, because she came from the ends of the earth to hear the wisdom of Solomon; and behold, something greater than Solomon is here (Matthew 12:42).

When Solomon asked God for "an understanding heart to judge Your people to discern between good and evil," God replied,

> behold, I have done according to your words. Behold, I have given you a wise and discerning heart, so that there has been no one like you before you, nor shall one like you arise after you (1 Kings 3:9, 12).

Yes, I know that Solomon forsook his great wisdom in his old age, but the fact remains that God said no one else would ever have such wisdom as he. Who, then, has the right to claim that he is wiser than the wisest man?

Greater than the most successful prophet, wiser than King Solomon—the next rungs up the ladder leave even these far behind.

Greater Than the Holy Sabbath

Because the Jews of Jesus' day were fanatical about Sabbath observance, they had added numerous traditions to the simple Sabbath commandment of the Old Testament. Jesus regularly flouted their traditions, but

He went even further when He claimed to be superior to the Sabbath.

> At that time Jesus went through the grainfields on the Sabbath, and His disciples became hungry and began to pick the heads of grain and eat. But when the Pharisees saw this, they said to Him, "Look, Your disciples do what is not lawful to do on a Sabbath" (Matthew 12:1-2).

According to Deuteronomy 23:25, it was perfectly all right to pluck the heads of standing grain in a neighbor's field. Using a sickle to cut the stalks was stealing. Eating a few grains out of one's hand was not. The Pharisees charged the disciples of Jesus not with stealing, but with working on the Sabbath. How serious was that accusation? The Old Testament Law was clear.

> Therefore you are to observe the sabbath, for it is holy to you. Everyone who profanes it shall surely be put to death; for whoever does any work on it, that person shall be cut off from among his people. For six days work may be done, but on the seventh day there is a sabbath of complete rest, holy to the LORD; whoever does any work on the sabbath day shall surely be put to death (Exodus 31:14-15).

The Jews of Jesus day, living under Roman rule, did not have the freedom to carry out the letter of the Old Testament law, but shortly after Moses announced the penalty an Israelite man decided to put it to the test. Isn't there always someone like that, pushing the boundaries just to see if they will hold?

> Now while the sons of Israel were in the wilderness, they found a man gathering wood on the sabbath day. Those who found him gathering wood brought him to Moses and Aaron and to all the congregation; and they put him

in custody because it had not been declared what should be done to him. Then the LORD said to Moses, "The man shall surely be put to death; all the congregation shall stone him with stones outside the camp." So all the congregation brought him outside the camp and stoned him to death with stones, just as the LORD had commanded Moses (Numbers 15:32-36).

Working on the Sabbath was a serious charge! How did Jesus defend His disciples? His answer is two-fold. First, He argued that human need and necessary work take precedence over God-ordained ceremonial regulations. David, in a time of need, ate the "consecrated bread, which was not lawful for him to eat nor for those with him, but for the priests alone" (Matthew 12:4) Even the priests had to do work in the temple on the Sabbath (Matthew 12:5). To reinforce His point, Jesus quoted from Hosea 6: "But if you had known what this means, 'I desire compassion and not a sacrifice,' you would not have condemned the innocent (Matthew 12:7).

Jesus used this kind of argument on other occasions to defend healing the sick on the Sabbath.

> And He said to them, "What man is there among you who has a sheep, and if it falls into a pit on the Sabbath, will he not take hold of it and lift it out? How much more valuable then is a man than a sheep! So then, it is lawful to do good on the Sabbath" (Matthew 12:11-12).

If Jesus had stopped at this point, He would have appeared to be just another rabbi making an argument on the basis of Old Testament texts. However, He didn't stop. He took a giant step up, passing over several rungs on our metaphorical ladder when He said, "For the Son of Man is Lord of the Sabbath" (Matthew 12:8).

"The Son of Man" was Jesus' normal way of referring to Himself. At the very least, He was claiming to have the authority to rule on acceptable Sabbath behavior. More than that, if He was the Lord of the Sabbath, His authority exceeded the authority of Moses who had to go ask Yahweh what to do with the man gathering sticks on the Sabbath. Finally, by implication, Jesus had the authority to set aside the Sabbath altogether, which His apostles later did (Colossians 2:16-17). Wow! And if that didn't light a fire under the Pharisees' fringed robes, Jesus had one more incendiary bomb to drop.

Greater Than the Holy Temple

Just after referring to the priests working in the temple on the Sabbath, Jesus added, "But I say to you that something greater than the temple is here" (Matthew 12:6).

Something greater than the temple? I can imagine the Pharisees looking all around for something or other greater than the temple: It's not over there on the left. It's not over there on the right. It's not behind us. Jesus must be talking about Himself!

What could be greater than the temple? The temple was the dwelling place of God on earth among His people, Israel. The Psalms are filled with longing for God's house because godly Israelites were deeply conscious of God's presence in the dark, inner recesses of the temple. Psalm 26:8 is typical: "O LORD, I love the habitation of Your house and the place where Your glory dwells."

Jesus is greater than the temple made of stone because He is the living temple, the ultimate dwelling place of Yahweh. Early in His ministry, Jesus proclaimed, "Destroy this temple, and in three days I will raise it up." That was sufficiently cryptic to confuse everybody who heard Him, but the apostle John writing after the resurrection of Jesus explained, "But He was speaking of the temple of His body" (John 2:19, 21).

When Jesus told the Pharisees that He was greater than the temple, they would not have been able to understand the full implication of His statement. They certainly understood, however, that He was claiming to be higher and holier than the holiest spot on earth. Perhaps it was not a direct claim to deity, but Jesus was standing confidently on the highest rung of the ladder with one end touching the earth and the other in heaven. The only way He could have been clearer would have been to shout, "Hey, you guys! I'm God."

The Humble Greatness of Jesus

There is one more thing to note, something that throws these "greater than" claims into sharp relief. Jesus is not only greater than Jonah, greater than Solomon, greater than the temple, and Lord of the

Sabbath. But He also said, "I am gentle and humble in heart" (Matthew 11:29).

Egomaniacs might tout their pretended humility in order to further their evil plans. Uriah Heep in Dickins' novel *David Copperfield* comes to mind. But what shall we say about Jesus? Either Jesus was fooling Himself, or He was fooling His disciples, or He was supremely conscious of His own voluntary lowering of Himself.

His disciples called Him "Teacher and Lord" and He said, "you are right, for so I am" (John 13:13), but then He lowered Himself to wash His disciples' feet. Perhaps a couple of weeks before that, as He was preparing His disciples for the cross that lay in His future, He said to His disciples,

> You know that those who are recognized as rulers of the Gentiles lord it over them; and their great men exercise authority over them. But it is not this way among you, but whoever wishes to become great among you shall be your servant; and whoever wishes to be first among you shall be slave of all. For even the Son of Man did not come to be served, but to serve, and to give His life a ransom for many (Mark 10:42-45).

From this perspective, Jesus is the greatest and the first because He humbly and willingly gave His life as a ransom for many.

Do you want to be great in God's kingdom? Learn to be the servant of all.

Chapter 6

The Son Sayings

In the last week of His earthly ministry, Jesus deliberately provoked the religious leaders who were already seeking an excuse and an opportunity to put Him to death. At His Jewish trial, after several failed attempts to find consistent witnesses against Him, the high priest finally asked Him straight out,

> "Are You the Christ, the Son of the Blessed One?" And Jesus said, "I am; and you shall see the Son of Man sitting at the right hand of Power, and coming with the clouds of heaven." Tearing his clothes, the high priest said, "What further need do we have of witnesses? "You have heard the blasphemy; how does it seem to you?" And they all condemned Him to be deserving of death (Mark 14:61-64).

Jesus confessed that He was the Son of God, and He identified Himself with the heavenly Son of Man prophesied in Daniel 7. In Matthew's account after Jesus had remained silent in the face of His accusers, the high priest placed Jesus under oath, saying "I adjure You by the living God, that You tell us whether You are the Christ, the Son of God" (26:63). To which Jesus answered, "You have said it yourself" (v. 64).

The Jewish leaders knew that Jesus claimed to be the Son of God, but prior to His trial they had trouble making the charge stick because He had recently couched this teaching in stories about an only son. The "son parables" were clear enough to the Pharisees even if obtuse modern professors don't seem to get them.

The Parable of the Vineyard

In the first of these parables just a few days before Jesus' trial, a landowner, "planted a vineyard and put a wall around it and dug a wine press in it, and built a tower" (Matthew 21:33). This is a reference to a familiar parable in Isaiah where the Lord's vineyard is Israel and Judah (Isaiah 5:1-7). The planting, the tower and the wine press are common to both parables. In Isaiah, the Lord is angry because His vineyard produced only worthless grapes. In the parable of Jesus, the master of the vineyard is angry for a different reason.

The master rented out his vineyard to share-croppers and went on a long journey. When the time of harvest came, he sent servants to collect his share of the crop.

> The vine-growers took his slaves and beat one, and killed another, and stoned a third. Again he sent another group of slaves larger than the first; and they did the same thing to them. But afterward he sent his son to them, saying, "They will respect my son." But when the vine-growers saw the son, they said among themselves, "This is the heir; come, let us kill him and seize his inheritance." They took him, and threw him out of the vineyard and killed him (Mathew 21:35-39).

When Jesus asked what the landowner will do, the religious leaders responded that he will kill those wretches and rent out his vineyard to more faithful sharecroppers. At this point, Jesus makes the application clear enough for even the dullest Pharisee to follow.

> Jesus said to them, "Did you never read in the Scriptures,
>> 'The stone which the builders rejected,
>> This became the chief corner *stone*;
>> This came about from the Lord,
>> And it is marvelous in our eyes'?
> Therefore I say to you, the kingdom of God will be taken away from you and given to a people, producing the fruit of it" (Matthew 21:42-43).

Not surprisingly, "When the chief priests and the Pharisees heard His parables, they understood that He was speaking about them" (v. 45). The landowner is God. The vineyard is the visible people of God. The sharecroppers are the unfaithful leaders who persecuted and killed the former prophets sent by God. The landowner's son is Jesus, whom the priests and Pharisees were already seeking to capture and kill. "When they sought to seize Him, they feared the people, because they considered Him to be a prophet" (v. 46). By the end of the week, their fury would overcome their fear.

The Parable of the Wedding Feast

The second "son parable" continues the theme of rejection.

> The kingdom of heaven may be compared to a king who gave a wedding feast for his son. And he sent out his slaves to call those who had been invited to the wedding feast, and they were unwilling to come (Matthew 22:2-3).

Some of the invited guests merely gave flimsy excuses, but others "seized his slaves and killed them" (v. 6). The enraged king then "destroyed those murderers and set their city on fire" (v. 7). Jesus had wept over the impending destruction of Jerusalem a few days earlier (Luke 19:41-44), and it loomed large in His private teaching to His disciples a day or two later (Luke 21:5-6).

As in the parable of the vineyard, the feast is given to other guests. The evil and the good are clothed in wedding garments to make an acceptable appearance at the table. In spite of the host's generosity, one guest has refused the offered wedding garment, and he is cast "into the outer darkness; in that place there will be weeping and gnashing of teeth." The conclusion of the matter is that "many are called, but few are chosen" (Matthew 22:13-14).

As a follow-up to the parable of the vineyard, it is obvious that the king is God, and His Son is Jesus. The Jews are the guests who refused to come, and the people that the Jews despise (Gentiles) are the happy ones feasting at the table of God. (See also Matthew 8:11-12 for the same teaching.)

The religious leaders clearly understood all of these things, so "Then the Pharisees went and plotted how they might trap Him in what He said" (Matthew 22:15).

The Greater Son of David

First the Pharisees, then the Sadducees, and then the Pharisees again tried to trick Jesus into discrediting Himself before the crowds. When they failed, Jesus posed a question that they could not answer.

> Now while the Pharisees were gathered together, Jesus asked them a question: "What do you think about the Christ, whose son is He?" They said to Him, "The son of David." He said to them, "Then how does David in the Spirit call Him 'Lord,' saying, 'The Lord said to my Lord, "Sit at My right hand, Until I put Your enemies beneath Your feet"'? If David then calls Him 'Lord,' how is He his son?" No one was able to answer Him a word, nor did anyone dare from that day on to ask Him another question (Matthew 22:41-46).

The quotation comes from Psalm 110, acknowledged by both Jews and Christians to be a messianic Psalm. In Jewish thinking, a son should pay homage to his father, not the other way around. How could a father ever call his son my Lord, meaning my master, my superior?

Jesus was not suggesting that Messiah was not descended from David. He was arguing that Messiah must be more than merely human, a conclusion implied in the psalm itself. In verse one, the Lord Messiah sits at Yahweh's right hand. In verse five, God is at Messiah's right hand. The positions seem to be interchangeable.

Not only that, but Messiah combines in Himself two roles that were never united in Israel. He is a king, and He has an eternal priesthood after the order of Melchizedek (v. 4).

The Pharisees probably did not understand everything that was implied in Jesus' argument, but in the light of His previous "Son parables" they might have grasped the two main points Jesus was making: First, Messiah, the son of David was far greater than David. Therefore, it was appropriate for David to call Him Lord. Second, they might have grasped that Jesus was making this claim for Himself.

If so, when the text says, "No one was able to answer Him a word," it may not mean that they were totally confused (v. 46). It may mean that they were unwilling to state the obvious.

Jesus before the Sanhedrin

The obvious finally came out in the demand of the high priest at Jesus' trial, "I adjure you [that is, *I charge you under oath*] by the living God, that you tell us whether You are the Christ, the Son of God" (Mathew 26:63).

Jesus answered in the affirmative: "You have said it yourself" (v. 64), "I am" (Mark 14:62). Then, to make sure His accusers had enough to crucify Him, He added, "hereafter you will see the Son of Man sitting at the right hand of Power, and coming on the clouds of heaven" (Matthew 26:64).

Jesus' answer combined quotations from two messianic Old Testament passages. The first is Psalm 110:1 where the King with an eternal priesthood sits at God's right hand. The second is Daniel 7:13-14.

> I kept looking in the night visions,
> And behold, with the clouds of heaven
> One like a Son of Man was coming,
> And He came up to the Ancient of Days
> And was presented before Him.
> And to Him was given dominion,
> Glory and a kingdom,
> That all the peoples, nations and men of every
>   language
> Might serve Him.
> His dominion is an everlasting dominion
> Which will not pass away;
> And His kingdom is one
> Which will not be destroyed.

Several features of this prophecy deserve comment. First, is the phrase, "One like a Son of Man." In Hebrew, "a son of man" simply means a human being. This heavenly figure is "like" a son of man. In other words, He appears in human form. Second, this Person in human form receives an everlasting dominion. It is *His* kingdom, not the kingdom of His descendants. He will personally be a king forever (just as He will be a priest forever, Psalm 110:4). Third, this kingly figure comes with the clouds of heaven. In the Old Testament only God comes in, with, or on the clouds (Psalm 97:2; 104:3; Isaiah 19:1; Nahum 1:3). So in this passage, we see a divine figure coming to the Ancient of Days.

Even though the Jews interpreted Daniel 7 as a prophecy of the messianic kingdom to come, they were not prepared to accept an ordinary looking man as somehow divine. Jesus consistently referred to Himself as "the Son of Man," but that phrase was ambiguous. Perhaps He was simply claiming to be a prophet, since God had called the prophet Ezekiel "son of man" ninety-three times. However, when Jesus claimed that the members of the Sanhedrin would see Him coming on the clouds of heaven, the high priest cried out, "He has blasphemed" (Matthew 26:65)!

The high priest appears to have gotten more from Jesus than he expected. If Jesus had only admitted He was the Son of God, as the high priest asked Him under oath, the Sanhedrin would have understood Him to be claiming to be the Messiah, Israel's rightful king. (See the next chapter for a further explanation.) That would have been enough to accuse Him before Pilate as a dangerous rival to the Roman emperor. As a matter of fact, that was the crime for which He was condemned and crucified.

When Jesus said He would come on the clouds of heaven, the high priest rightly understood His words to be a claim to divinity. Hence, his outraged exclamation, "He has blasphemed!"

In the last days before His crucifixion, Jesus presented Himself as the beloved Son of the Father, as the greater Son of David, and as the divine Son of Man who would one day come on the clouds to receive an everlasting kingdom.

The Jews hated Jesus for claiming to be what my professor insisted Jesus had never said He was: the divine Son of God.

Chapter 7

Son of God in John

As noted in the previous chapter, the religious leaders had so much trouble producing consistent witnesses at Jesus' trial that they finally resorted to forcing a confession from the prisoner Himself. In the last week of His life on earth, Jesus used parables to teach that He was the Son of God. However, much earlier than this, in the gospel of John, He taught the same truth more plainly.

That raises a significant question. Why was it such a big deal for Peter to confess that Jesus was the Son of God in Matthew 16? Nathanael had already done that in John 1:49 as Jesus was beginning His public ministry. Let's begin with what the words meant on Nathanael's lips.

The Messianic Son

"Son of God" was a first-century title for the Messiah based on a number of Old Testament passages. God promised David that He would establish a kingdom ruled by David's descendants. Regarding the Davidic king the Lord said, "I will be a father to him and he will be a son to Me" (2 Samuel 7:14). Therefore, the kings of David's line were regarded as adopted sons of God.[±]

Time and time again, the Davidic kings failed to live up to their calling. Aside from a few good kings and a couple of great ones, the general tendency was downhill. Disobedience led to judgment, and the last king of David's line died in Babylon in the sixth century BC.

Even before that time, the prophets of Israel began looking forward to one great king in whom God's promise to David would be fulfilled: "Your house and your kingdom shall endure before Me forever; you throne shall be established forever" (2 Samuel 7:16). This king came to be called the Messiah (Messiah means Anointed One), and He would be the Son of God *par excellence.*

In Psalm 2, the kings of the earth "take counsel together against the LORD and against His Anointed" (v. 2). God mocks them and says to His Anointed, "You are my Son, today I have begotten You" (v. 7). This verse is quoted or alluded to some ten times in the New Testament. On the basis of Psalm 2 and God's promise to David, the Jews of Jesus' day used "Son of God" as equivalent to "Messiah."

[±] It is interesting, however, that we do not find the title, "son of God" used for David's descendants in the books of Kings and Chronicles. Perhaps the messianic implications of the promise quickly overshadowed any other usage.

When John baptized Jesus, he heard the Father speaking from heaven saying, "This is My beloved Son, in whom I am well-pleased" (Matthew 3:17). Therefore, after John had pointed Jesus out as the one whose coming he was sent to announce, it is not surprising that one of John's followers would say to Jesus, "Rabbi, You are the Son of God; You are the King of Israel" (John 1:49).

At this stage of Jesus' ministry, the title Son of God in the mouth of His disciples meant no more than that He was a human Messiah. However, it soon came to mean much more to them because Jesus Himself used it in a higher sense.

The Son and the Sabbath

One Sabbath day in Jerusalem, Jesus found a man who had been incapacitated for thirty-eight years. After healing him, Jesus told him to pick up his pallet and walk. Carrying anything outside one's house was strictly forbidden on the Sabbath, so the Jews added this to the list of Jesus' Sabbath violations.

> But He answered them, "My Father is working until now, and I Myself am working." For this reason therefore the Jews were seeking all the more to kill Him, because He not only was breaking the Sabbath, but also was calling God His own Father, making Himself equal with God (John 5:17-18).

Jews of Jesus' day did not address God as "My Father." He was the father of the nation (Exodus 4:22), but individual Jews did not presume to have a father/son kind of intimacy with God. Still, why did the Jews conclude that Jesus was making Himself equal with God?

The answer lies in Jesus' observation that God works on the Sabbath. It is true that God finished His creative work after the sixth day, but His providential work continues. He sustains the world and its operations moment by moment. The Jewish rabbis actually discussed the problem of God's working on the Sabbath. Some suggested that He had the right to break His own rules. Others said that since the whole universe was God's house, He was not really breaking the Sabbath since He wasn't carrying anything out of His house (Carson, 247).

Jesus claimed to have such a relationship to God that whatever rationale the Jews might give for God's work on the Sabbath would apply equally to Him. No mere man could make such a claim. Therefore, Jesus was claiming to be divine. That is what the Jews concluded.

My first observation regarding this incident is that we have seen something like it before when Jesus said that He was the "Lord of the Sabbath" and greater than the temple (Matthew 12). In Matthew 12 and John 5, Jesus claims the right both to work on the Sabbath and to give others permission to do the same, which would be bold-faced hubris if it were not true.

My second observation on John 5 is that Jesus had a golden opportunity deny His equality with the Father.

He didn't. Instead, He added fuel to the fire of the Jews' hatred. He made claims that could only be true if He were the Son of God by nature, not just by adoption:

➢ The Son gives life to whom He wishes (v. 21);

➢ The Son will judge all men (v. 22);

➢ The Son receives the same honor as the Father (v. 23);

➢ The Son has life in Himself (that is, He sustains His own life) as the Father does (v. 26);

➢ The Son will raise the dead (vv. 25-29).

Who is this Son? He is the Son of God (v. 25), and to make sure His hearers got the point, Jesus used His well-known self-designation, "He is the Son of Man" (27).

On a subsequent visit to Jerusalem, Jesus again highlighted His unique relationship to the Father when He said, "I and My Father are one" (John 10:30). Immediately, "The Jews picked up stones to stone Him" because, they said, "You, being a man, make yourself out to be God" (vv. 31, 33). Jesus noted that even human judges are occasionally called gods in the Old Testament (v. 34, quoting Psalm 82:6). Therefore, His exalted status, as the One sanctified and sent into the world by the Father, warranted His calling Himself the Son of God. Jesus specifically confessed that their accusation was correct: "I said, 'I am the Son of God'" (John 10:36).

Finally, to make it clear that His unity with the Father was not just a unity of purpose, Jesus added, "the Father is in Me, and I in the Father. Therefore they were seeking again to seize Him, and He eluded their grasp" (John 10:38-39).

This chapter began by asking why Peter's confession in Matthew 16 was such a big deal since Nathanael had called Jesus the Son of God much earlier in John 1. The answer is that "Son of God" had taken on a much deeper meaning by the time Jesus asked His disciples, "But who do you say that I am?" (Matthew 16:15). The disciples had certainly heard Jesus' interchange with the Jews in John 5. They had heard Him forgive sins; seen Him miraculously feed 9,000 men (5,000, then 4,000 more); watched Him walk on the boisterous, wind-blown Sea of Galilee; and heal all manner of diseases.

So, when Peter boldly answered, "You are the Christ, the Son of the living God," he was not repeating something he might have heard from John the Baptist. He was speaking out of a wealth of personal experience. Not only that, but in view of John 5, Peter apparently sensed, at least dimly, that Jesus was somehow divine. Otherwise, we are at a loss to explain Jesus' strong endorsement of his confession: "Blessed are you, Simon Barjona, because flesh and blood did not reveal this to you, but My Father who is in heaven" (Matthew 16:16-17).

Though Jesus claimed to be the Son of God, no one is able truly to accept Jesus as Lord and God unless the Father reveals it to his heart as He did to Simon Peer. If you do not yet believe that Christ is the Son of God, why not ask the Father to reveal to you whether it is so.

Chapter 8

Living Water

Up until the previous chapter I have limited myself to occasional references to the gospel of John. I refrained because some people claim that John's gospel presents a different picture of Jesus than the synoptic gospels (Matthew, Mark, Luke) do. However, as we have seen, Jesus' self-identification is just as bold in the other gospels as it is in John. In this and the next few chapters, we will examine some of the remarkable things our Lord said about Himself as recorded in the fourth gospel.

Living Water Sayings

When Jesus met a Samaritan woman at Jacob's well, He offered her living water, saying,

> If you knew the gift of God, and who it is who says to you, "Give me a drink," you would have asked Him, and He would have given you living water.... Everyone who drinks of this water [from Jacob's well] will thirst again; but whoever drinks of the water that I will give him shall never thirst; but the water that I will give him will become in him a well of water springing up to eternal life (John 4:13-14).

A year or two later, Jesus used the same imagery at the close of the Feast of Tabernacles. During the feast, it had become customary for the High Priest to fill a golden pitcher with water from the pool of Siloam and to carry it in procession back to the temple where it was poured out before the Lord. "These ceremonies... were related in Jewish thought both to the LORD'S provision of water in the desert [Exodus 17; Numbers 20] and to the LORD'S pouring out of the Spirit in the last days (Carson 322)." The water-pouring ceremony of the feast appears to be the backdrop for another Living Water pronouncement by the Lord.

> Now on the last day, the great day of the feast, Jesus stood and cried out, saying, "If anyone is thirsty, let him come to Me and drink. He who believes in Me, as the Scripture said, 'From his innermost being will flow rivers of living water.'" But this He spoke of the Spirit, whom those who believed in Him were to receive; for the Spirit was not yet given, because Jesus was not yet glorified (John 7:37-39).

In these living water sayings, Jesus associates Himself and His ministry with a host of Old Testament pronouncements and prophecies.

Old Testament Parallels

First, Jesus claims to be the source of living water. In Jeremiah 2, the LORD accuses Israel of forsaking Him to worship the false gods of the nations. He provides fresh water; other gods only offer muddy sludge at the bottom of a pit:

> For My people have committed two evils:
> They have forsaken Me,
> The fountain of living waters,
> To hew for themselves cisterns,
> Broken cisterns
> That can hold no water (v. 13).

If Jesus is not Yahweh, He is a broken cistern, a false god who has nothing to offer.

What is this living water? *Living water* is the Hebrew idiom equivalent to English *running water*. Of course, water is no more alive than it has feet with which to run, but both idioms aptly describe the movement of flowing water as opposed to still water in a pond, a well or a cistern. That is the picture in Jeremiah 2:13.

The phrase *living water* also suggests water that is life giving, which is the way Jesus used the idiom in John 4. The water He gives springs up inside of a person resulting in eternal life. Jesus therefore claimed to be able to impart eternal life to those who receive living water from Him.

We find the idea of life-giving water in Ezekiel's vision of the coming messianic kingdom. The glory of God that left the temple before the Babylonian captivity (Ezekiel 9-11) will return to fill the messianic temple (Ezekiel 43). From the presence of God in the temple, an ever-deepening stream will flow out toward the Dead Sea. (The Dead Sea is so named because no fish or plants live in it.) When the waters from God's presence in the temple reach the sea,

The waters of the sea become fresh. It will come about that every living creature which swarms in every place where the river goes, will live. And there will be very many fish, for these waters go there and the others become fresh; so everything will live where the river goes (Ezekiel 47:8-9).

While the final fulfillment of this prophecy awaits the second coming of Christ, Jesus implied that He was at least a preliminary fulfillment of it. In John 2, Jesus described His body as the temple of God (vv. 19-22). In John 4 and 7, the life-giving water comes from Him as it does from the temple in Ezekiel 47.

As noted earlier, the water-pouring ceremony at the Feast of Tabernacles looked forward to the outpouring of God's Spirit in the last days. While the disciples did not link living water with the out-poured Spirit until after Pentecost, it seems clear from the Old Testament prophecies that Jesus intended them to make that connection.

When Jesus invited the Samaritan woman at the well and later the people at the feast to drink from Him, He was echoing the Old Testament invitation of God.

Ho! Every one who thirsts, come to the waters; And you who have no money come, buy and eat.
Come, buy wine and milk
Without money and without cost (Isaiah 55:1).

The afflicted and needy are seeking water, but there
is none,
And their tongue is parched with thirst;
I, the LORD, will answer them Myself,
As the God of Israel I will not forsake them.
I will open rivers on the bare heights
And springs in the midst of the valleys;

> I will make the wilderness a pool of water
> And the dry land fountains of water
> (Isaiah 41:17-18).

The water that will satisfy the thirst of God's people in the last days is His Holy Spirit:

> For I will pour out water on the thirsty *land*
> And streams on the dry ground;
> I will pour out My Spirit on your offspring
> And My blessing on your descendants;
> And they will spring up among the grass
> Like poplars by streams of water (Isaiah 44:3-4).

Joel's predictions regarding the day of the Lord make the same connection between the out-poured Spirit and refreshing water.

> It will come about after this
> That I will pour out My Spirit on all mankind;
> And your sons and daughters will prophesy,
> Your old men will dream dreams,
> Your young men will see visions.
> Even on the male and female servants
> I will pour out My Spirit in those days
> (Joel 2:28-29).

Peter quoted this passage when the Spirit came from Christ upon the church (Acts 2). A little later in his prophecy, Joel adds:

> And in that day
> The mountains will drip with sweet wine,
> And the hills will flow with milk,
> And all the brooks of Judah will flow with water;
> And a spring will go out from the house of the
>   LORD
> To water the valley of Shittim (Joel 3:18).

"The valley of *Shittim* is the barren valley of the Jordan, above the Dead Sea,"(Keil 230) and this accords with the prophecy of Ezekiel 47 quoted above.

So, the Old Testament prophets link the outpouring of the Spirit with rivers of water that bring life and refreshment. In the upper room discourse, Jesus gave further confirmation that the promise of living water (John 4 and 7) would be fulfilled by the coming of the Spirit. On the night before His crucifixion, Jesus said that He would send the Holy Spirit from the Father after He (Jesus) went away (John 14:16-18, 26; 16:7-15).

The traditional ceremonies at the Feast of Tabernacles linked the pouring of water with the future outpouring of the Spirit. Since Jesus gave His living-water promise at that feast; and since the prophets make the same linkage; and since Jesus predicted the coming of the Spirit after His death, we conclude that John understood his Master properly when he wrote,

> But this He spoke of the Spirit, whom those who believed in Him were to receive; for the Spirit was not yet given, because Jesus was not yet glorified (John 7:39).

To summarize:

- ➤ Yahweh alone gives living water to those who thirst.

- ➤ This living water is an emblem of His Spirit.

- ➤ Yahweh alone pours out His Spirit.

> ➢ Jesus gives the living water of the Spirit to those who thirst.

> ➢ Therefore, Jesus is Yahweh.

What are these soul thirsts that Jesus offers to quench? They are the same as the burdens Jesus offered to lift when He promised rest and peace to the heavy laden (Matthew 11:28-30). Our sins not only weigh us down, but they also leave us unsatisfied and empty. As we have seen in the synoptic gospels, Jesus forgives repentant sinners. Trials and troubles burden our souls and fill us with doubt and despair until we open up our hearts to the peace Jesus offers (John 14:27; 16:33). Our world feels dark and our future without purpose until Jesus opens our eyes to see His glory in the gospel and the glory we will share when we see Him (John 17:22-24).

Does this describe you? Will you humble yourself and come to Jesus for the living water that saves eternally and satisfies continually?

Chapter 9

The Good Shepherd

$-\backsim-$

In the gospels, Jesus describes Himself as a shepherd who seeks His lost sheep, defends them from their enemies, and knows them intimately and individually. These are actions ascribed to God as the shepherd of His people in the Old Testament.

Jesus Finds His Sheep

In the synoptic gospels, Jesus presents Himself as the Shepherd who seeks His lost sheep. In Luke 15, the Pharisees were grumbling, saying about Jesus, "This man receives sinners and eats with them" (v. 2). Their criticism provided the platform from which Jesus launched three well-known parables—the lost sheep; the lost coin; and the lost son (usually called the prodigal son).

In the first parable, Jesus defends His ministry to sinners by presenting Himself as the one who seeks the lost.

> What man among you, if he has a hundred sheep and has lost one of them, does not leave the ninety-nine in the open pasture and go after the one which is lost until he

finds it? When he has found it, he lays it on his shoulders, rejoicing. And when he comes home, he calls together his friends and his neighbors, saying to them, "Rejoice with me, for I have found my sheep which was lost!" I tell you that in the same way, there will be *more* joy in heaven over one sinner who repents than over ninety-nine righteous persons who need no repentance (Luke 15:4-7).

Who is this shepherd, who seeks the lost? The context implies that it is Jesus. The story of Zaccheus confirms this conclusion. When the religious leaders grumbled (again!) because Jesus was eating with sinners, the Lord said, "For the Son of Man has come to seek and to save that which was lost" (Luke 19:10).

For Old Testament parallels, I begin with Psalm 119:176 where the writer prays,

> I have gone astray like a lost sheep; seek Your
>   servant,
> For I do not forget your commandments.

God is the one who seeks His lost sheep.

In Ezekiel 34, God reproves the unworthy shepherds of God's flock—the princes, the priests, and the false prophets of Israel. He says,

> Those who are sickly you have not strengthened, the diseased you have not healed, the broken you have not bound up, the scattered you have not brought back, nor have you sought for the lost; but with force and with severity you have dominated them.... My flock wandered through all the mountains and on every high hill; My flock was scattered over all the surface of the earth, and there was no one to search or seek *for them* (Ezekiel 34:4, 6).

What is the remedy for this dreadful neglect of the lost sheep?

> For thus says the Lord GOD, "Behold, I Myself will search for My sheep and seek them out. As a shepherd cares for his herd in the day when he is among his scattered sheep, so I will care for My sheep and will deliver them from all the places to which they were scattered on a cloudy and gloomy day" (Ezekiel 34:11-12).

The Lord assigns the task of gathering His sheep to Himself—just as Jesus does in Luke 15.

Jesus cares for His sheep

More familiar than either Psalm 119 or Ezekiel is the well-beloved Psalm 23:

> The LORD is my shepherd,
> I shall not want (v. 1).

This good shepherd leads, feeds, and protects His sheep (vv. 2-5). He anoints the sheep's head with oil (v. 5), probably as a salve for a wound or as protection against flies and scab. For David, of course, the anointing recalled the day that Samuel anointed him to be the next king of Israel. Along with the anointing of oil came an anointing by the Holy Spirit (1 Samuel 16:13). Finally, the contented sheep exclaims,

> Surely goodness and lovingkindness will follow me
>   all the days of my life,
> And I will dwell in the house of the LORD forever
>   (v. 6).

The sheep looks forward to the security of the shepherd's house after a season of wandering in the pastures, and David looks forward to eternal life in the house of the Lord.

Psalm 23 and Ezekiel 34 provide essential background for another well-known passage, John 10, in which Jesus describes Himself as the good shepherd (v. 14). In this chapter, Jesus deliberately contrasts Himself to the Jewish leaders who had just proven themselves to be false shepherds.

In John 9, when Jesus gave sight to a man born blind, the Jewish leaders said that Jesus must be a sinner because He broke their law by healing on the Sabbath. The formerly blind man defended Jesus and insisted that He must have come from God. Though the Jews could not deny that a remarkable miracle had happened, they vented their irrational fury against Jesus by excommunicating the man who had been healed. Later that day as Jesus was talking with the man about spiritual blindness, some Pharisees standing by said, "'We are not blind too, are we?' Jesus said to them, 'If you were blind, you would have no sin; but since you say, "We see," your sin remains'" (John 9:40-41). These are the false shepherds Jesus attacks in the next chapter.

Just as the leaders of Israel were false shepherds in Ezekiel's day, so Jesus levels the same accusation against the Jewish leaders of His day.

> Truly, truly, I say to you, he who does not enter by the door into the fold of the sheep, but climbs up some other

way, he is a thief and a robber. But he who enters by the door is a shepherd of the sheep (John 10:1-2).

All who came before Me are thieves and robbers, but the sheep did not hear them (v. 8).

The thief comes only to steal and kill and destroy; I came that they may have life, and have *it* abundantly (v. 10).

What are the characteristics of the good shepherd, Jesus Christ? As in Psalm 23, Jesus leads His sheep.

> But he who enters by the door is a shepherd of the sheep. To him the doorkeeper opens, and the sheep hear his voice, and he calls his own sheep by name and leads them out. When he puts forth all his own, he goes ahead of them, and the sheep follow him because they know his voice. A stranger they simply will not follow, but will flee from him, because they do not know the voice of strangers (John 10:2-5).

Travelers in the Near East before the advent of modernity had occasion to watch shepherds calling their individual flocks out of a larger herd. Even when a stranger wore the shepherd's clothes and imitated his unique call, the sheep would avoid him.

How is Jesus able to lead His sheep? He knows them individually, and they know Him, and they know His voice (vv. 14, 27). Scripture frequently mentions this kind of mutual knowledge between God and His people (Jeremiah 31:34; Amos 3:2 [ESV]; 1 Corinthians 8:32; Galatians 4:8-9; Timothy 2:19). When we consider that Jesus' sheep include believers from outside the Jewish fold (John 10:16; 17:20), we must conclude that Jesus is claiming to have supernatural knowledge of a vast number of future followers.

Jesus protects His sheep

In the next section of His discourse, Jesus calls Himself the door of the sheep.

> So Jesus said to them again, "Truly, truly, I say to you, I am the door of the sheep.... I am the door; if anyone enters through Me, he will be saved, and will go in and out and find pasture (John 10:7, 9).

Some have supposed that Jesus here drops the metaphor of the shepherd. That is not necessary. Verses 1-3 picture a village sheepfold where several flocks might be kept together at night. Verses 7 and 9 may picture the small stone enclosures, many of them centuries old, which shepherds used when their flocks were far from any village. My wife and I saw one such enclosure when our tour bus traveled from Jericho to Jerusalem. These small sheepfolds had no door or gate, so the shepherd would lie down across the entrance at night. Thus, he became the door past whom the sheep would go out to pasture by day and come in to rest by night.

To be able to go in and out freely is an Old Testament expression that pictures safety and security. There are no enemies or dangers that would keep a person fearfully hiding in his house. He feels safe enough to go out to do his business and then to return to the comfortable shelter of his home. Jesus is claiming to provide that kind of security for His sheep, just as Yahweh does for His people.

> The LORD will protect you from all evil;
> He will keep your soul.
> The LORD will guard your going out and your

> coming in
> From this time forth and forever (Psalm 121:7-8).

So also Ezekiel 34 looks forward to the day when God's sheep

> will no longer be a prey to the nations, and the beasts of the earth will not devour them; but they will live securely, and no one will make *them* afraid (Ezekiel 34:28).

A shepherd's life in Bible times was dangerous. As a shepherd boy, David killed both a lion and a bear (1 Samuel 17:34-37). While a shepherd might risk his life for his sheep,

> He who is a hired hand, and not a shepherd, who is not the owner of the sheep, sees the wolf coming, and leaves the sheep and flees, and the wolf snatches them and scatters them. He *flees* because he is a hired hand and is not concerned about the sheep (John 10:12-13).

Jesus, however, did more than risk His life. He deliberately laid it down. For this reason, He is not *one* good shepherd among many. He is *the* good shepherd, the shepherd *par excellence.*

> I am the good shepherd; the good shepherd lays down His life for the sheep (v. 11).

> I am the good shepherd, and I know My own and My own know Me, even as the Father knows Me and I know the Father; and I lay down My life for the sheep (vv. 14-15).

> For this reason the Father loves Me, because I lay down My life so that I may take it again. No one has taken it away from Me, but I lay it down on My own initiative. I have authority to lay it down, and I have authority to take

it up again. This commandment I received from My Father (vv. 17-18).

Jesus is the ultimate defender of His sheep, first because He laid down His life for them, and second because He took up His life again. Our shepherd is not dead. He is alive.

Jesus is the divine Shepherd

Now I want to raise an objection which probably hasn't been bothering you. In the Old Testament, most of the time the Lord is the shepherd of His people. Occasionally, however, the Old Testament prophets speak of another shepherd alongside the Lord. Maybe Jesus is only claiming to be a subsidiary shepherd, a human shepherd under God. That suggestion, however, does not deal with all the evidence.

After the Lord promises to care for His people as a shepherd (Ezekiel 34:12), He says,

> Then I will set over them one shepherd, My servant David, and he will feed them; he will feed them himself and be their shepherd. And I, the LORD, will be their God, and My servant David will be prince among them; I the LORD have spoken (vv. 23-24).

> My servant David will be king over them, and they will all have one shepherd; and they will walk in My ordinances and keep My statutes and observe them. They will live on the land that I gave to Jacob My servant, in which your fathers lived; and they will live on it, they, and their sons and their sons' sons, forever; and David My servant will be their prince forever (Ezekiel 37:24-25).

The prophets sometimes call the future Messiah David (Jeremiah 30:9; Hosea 3:5). This is not a resurrected David, but a son, a child to be born of David's line who will sit upon his throne (Isaiah 9:6-7). In Isaiah's prophecy the son is the "Eternal Father," and there "will be no end to the increase of His government." Ezekiel concurs: "David My servant will be their prince forever."

In these passages, the Messiah, the shepherd and king of God's people, rules forever. He possesses one of the essential attributes of deity. Jesus claims no less for Himself. He is the one who is able to give eternal life and to protect them forever.

> My sheep hear My voice, and I know them, and they follow Me; and I give eternal life to them, and they will never perish; and no one will snatch them out of My hand. My Father, who has given them to Me, is greater than all; and no one is able to snatch them out of the Father's hand. I and the Father are one (John 10:27-30).

In view of the astounding promises He makes in these verses, Jesus' claim to be one with the Father must be a claim to essential deity. He is not merely one in purpose with the Father. He does exactly the same things as the Father does.

In Luke 15, Jesus claims to be the shepherd who seeks and finds His lost sheep. His implicit claim to deity in that passage becomes explicit in John chapter 10. He is the good shepherd because of His intimate knowledge of the sheep, because of His willingness and ability to lay down His life and to take it up again, because of His unity with the Father, and because He does the works that only God can do.

The Career of the Christ

— ❦ —

Jesus was born in Bethlehem about 5 BC (Yes, the medieval monk who devised the BC/AD convention made mistake.) His early years were spent in Nazareth working as a carpenter alongside His father, finally taking over the family business. When He was about 30, He began preaching and healing in Galilee, drawing sizeable crowds. Probably in AD 33, He was crucified on a trumped-up charge of rebellion against Rome.

That would be a fair summary of the life of Jesus from a secular, historical perspective. My question for this chapter is *how did Jesus see Himself and His career?* In the gospels Jesus looks back before His birth in Bethlehem and forward beyond His death to His resurrection and return.

A Unique Relationship with the Father

When God brought Israel out of bondage in Egypt, He said, "Israel is My son, My firstborn" (Exodus 4:22). This was a national designation mentioned occasionally by the prophets (Isaiah 63:16; 64:8; Jeremiah 31:9; Hosea 11:1). Individual Israelites were not encouraged to address God as Father, although the Davidic king could claim to be an adopted son of God (2 Samuel 7:14).

It was revolutionary, therefore, when Jesus taught His disciples to call God *Father*. As a child trusts his father to give him good gifts, so we are to trust our Father in heaven to give us what we need (Matthew 7:9-11).

Jesus claimed for Himself a still more intimate connection with the God. In fact, He claimed a unique relationship with the Father. When He sent the twelve to preach in hostile territory, He said,

> Therefore everyone who confesses Me before men, I will also confess him before My Father who is in heaven. But whoever denies Me before men, I will also deny him before My Father who is in heaven (Matthew 10:32-33).

None of us has the right to confess or deny another human being before our heavenly Father. Furthermore, God would not base His acceptance of any individual on that person's confession of allegiance to us.

When the cities where Jesus had done most of His miracles turned a cold shoulder to Him, He threatened them with a judgment more severe than that which fell on the land of Sodom. Who, then, will respond to the message of Christ? Not the wise or the privileged, but the weak and the insignificant.

> Yes, Father, for this way was well-pleasing in Your sight. All things have been handed over to Me by My

Father; and no one knows the Son except the Father; nor does anyone know the Father except the Son, and anyone to whom the Son wills to reveal Him (Matthew 11:26-27).

Jesus claimed a unique, personal knowledge of the Father, a knowledge that He had the right to impart to whomever He willed.

The Heavenly Origin of the Son

Jesus' special relationship to the Father appears in the sending of the Son. We have already looked at the parable in Matthew 21, in which the owner of a vineyard sent his son to collect the fruit from the sharecroppers. The theme of the Father sending the Son occurs occasionally in the synoptic gospels, and becomes prominent in the gospel of John. A few of these references hint at a heavenly origin of the Son who was with the Father before His birth in Bethlehem.

> Jesus said to them, "If God were your Father, you would love Me, for I proceeded forth and have come from God, for I have not even come on My own initiative, but He sent Me" (John 8:42).

> If he called them gods, to whom the word of God came (and the Scripture cannot be broken), do you say of Him, whom the Father sanctified and sent into the world, "You are blaspheming," because I said, "I am the Son of God" (John 10:35-36)?

Although "sent into the world" implies that Jesus came into the world from outside it, that conclusion is not necessary. (See the same language in John 17:18.) However, the heavenly origin of the Son is clinched in

Jesus' discourse on the bread of life following the feeding of the five thousand. Jesus said,

> For the bread of God is that which comes down out of heaven, and gives life to the world (John 6:33).

> I am the bread of life; he who comes to Me will not hunger, and he who believes in Me will never thirst (John 6:35).

> For I have come down from heaven, not to do My own will, but the will of Him who sent Me (John 6:38).

The Eternal Existence of the Son

The heavenly origin of Christ leads us to consider next Jesus' claim to have an eternal existence. In a sharp interchange with the Jews, Jesus said that these descendants of Abraham were, in fact, children of the devil (John 8:44). Naturally, they hated Him for this statement, but their rage boiled over when He claimed to have seen Abraham. Jesus said,

> "Your father Abraham rejoiced to see My day, and he saw *it* and was glad." So the Jews said to Him, "You are not yet fifty years old, and have You seen Abraham?" Jesus said to them, "Truly, truly, I say to you, before Abraham was born, I am." Therefore they picked up stones to throw at Him, but Jesus hid Himself and went out of the temple (John 8:56-59).

The phrase "I am" is normally followed by a noun or an adjective, as when Jesus said, "I am the door of the sheep" or "I am the good shepherd." In John 8:58 "I am" stands alone as it does in Exodus 3.

> Then Moses said to God, "Behold, I am going to the sons of Israel, and I will say to them, 'The God of your fathers has sent me to you.' Now they may say to me, 'What is

His name?' 'What shall I say to them?" God said to Moses, "I AM WHO I AM"; and He said, "Thus you shall say to the sons of Israel, 'I AM has sent me to you.'" God, furthermore, said to Moses, "Thus you shall say to the sons of Israel, 'The LORD [Yahweh], the God of your fathers, the God of Abraham, the God of Isaac, and the God of Jacob, has sent me to you.' This is My name forever, and this is My memorial-name to all generations (Exodus 3:13-15).±

The name Yahweh is derived from the Hebrew verb *to be*. I AM describes God as eternal, self-existing, and unchangeable. Everything else in the universe has come into being. God simply is. That is what the Jews understood Jesus to be claiming. That is the reason they wanted to stone Him for blasphemy.

The Jews were not mistaken. Jesus highlighted His eternal existence in a prayer uttered in the presence of His disciples on the night before His crucifixion: "Now, Father, glorify Me together with Yourself, with the glory which I had with You before the world was" (John 17:5). Though none of the other gospels specifically mentions the pre-temporal glory of Christ, all of them speak of His glorious return.

± Yahweh (usually LORD or GOD in English translations) was known from ancient times (Genesis 4:26). It was used by the patriarchs (Genesis 14:22; 15:2). However, the significance of the name had not yet been revealed. That is what the Lord meant when He said to Moses, "I appeared to Abraham, Isaac, and Jacob, as God Almighty, but by my name LORD, I did not make Myself known to them" (Exodus 6:3). For the patriarchs, Yahweh did not have a special covenant significance. In Exodus 3 God elevated the name Yahweh as His "memorial name to all generations."

Jesus Predicted His Own Future

Futurists are a dime a dozen. Successful predictors of the future aren't so cheap. No other prophet has ever done what Jesus did. He repeatedly predicted His own death and resurrection, and then He pulled it off. He also predicted His personal return to earth in glory.

After Peter's great confession that Jesus was the Christ, the Son of God,

> He began to teach them that the Son of Man must suffer many things and be rejected by the elders and the chief priests and the scribes, and be killed, and after three days rise again (Mark 8:31).

> From there they went out and *began* to go through Galilee, and He did not want anyone to know *about it*. For He was teaching His disciples and telling them, "The Son of Man is to be delivered into the hands of men, and they will kill Him; and when He has been killed, He will rise three days later." But they did not understand *this* statement, and they were afraid to ask Him (Mark 9:30-32).

> They were on the road going up to Jerusalem, and Jesus was walking on ahead of them; and they were amazed, and those who followed were fearful. And again He took the twelve aside and began to tell them what was going to happen to Him, *saying*, "Behold, we are going up to Jerusalem, and the Son of Man will be delivered to the chief priests and the scribes; and they will condemn Him to death and will hand Him over to the Gentiles. They will mock Him and spit on Him, and scourge Him and kill *Him*, and three days later He will rise again" (Mark 10:32-34).

With such abundant forewarning, why were the disciples so surprised when Jesus rose from the dead? Perhaps they hoped this was another one of His parables, but they were afraid to ask what it meant. Luke tells us that "this statement was hidden from them" (Luke 18:34). God did not want them to understand until the prediction came true. (I suspect that is also the case for us with the details of Christ's second coming.)

After predicting His death and resurrection, Jesus proceeded to declare that He would come again in glory.

> For whoever is ashamed of Me and My words in this adulterous and sinful generation, the Son of Man will also be ashamed of him when He comes in the glory of His Father with the holy angels (Mark 8:38).

> But in those days, after that tribulation, the sun will be darkened and the moon will not give its light, and the stars will be falling from heaven, and the powers that are in the heavens will be shaken. Then they will see the Son of Man coming in clouds with great power and glory (Mark 13:24-26).

Similar statements occur in Matthew and Luke. So while the synoptic gospels focus on the return of Christ in glory, the gospel of John draws our attention to the glory which Jesus had with the Father before the world began. These are complementary parts of the teaching of Jesus regarding His own person and His career.

Omnipresence

In a series of prophecies, Jesus predicted the formation and success of His church after His death and resurrection. Two striking aspects this prediction imply His omnipresence. First, He said that *He* would build His church. He did not say that His church would be built by others. Second, He promised that He would be present in and with His church. Let's look in a bit more detail at these predictions.

> I also say to you that you are Peter, and upon this rock I will build My church; and the gates of Hades will not overpower it. I will give you the keys of the kingdom of heaven; and whatever you bind on earth shall have been bound in heaven, and whatever you loose on earth shall have been loosed in heaven (Matthew 16:18-19).

The precise meaning of "on this rock" has been debated endlessly. Without getting into all the fine details, it is enough to note that Peter himself says that Jesus is the precious cornerstone on which the house of God is built (1 Peter 2:4-8).

The authority to bind and loose was not given only to Peter. It belongs to the whole church. Stubborn, flagrant sinners are to be brought before the church.

> If he refuses to listen to them, tell it to the church; and if he refuses to listen even to the church, let him be to you as a Gentile and a tax collector. Truly I say to you, whatever you bind on earth shall have been bound in heaven; and whatever you loose on earth shall have been loosed in heaven (Matthew 18:17-18).

Why is the church able to exercise this kind of authority? The reason is that Christ is present in His church.

> Again I say to you, that if two of you agree on earth about anything that they may ask, it shall be done for them by My Father who is in heaven. For where two or three have gathered together in My name, I am there in their midst (Matthew 18:19-20).

When the church is gathered in His name, properly organized and living under the word of God, the ever-present Jesus ratifies the disciplinary decisions of the church.

After His resurrection, Jesus spoke even more clearly about His continual presence with His people.

> Go therefore and make disciples of all the nations, baptizing them in the name of the Father and the Son and the Holy Spirit, teaching them to observe all that I commanded you; and lo, I am with you always, even to the end of the age (Matthew 28:19-20).

There is no hint in these predictions that Jesus would be with His church in some vague, non-personal way. It has become common to say that our departed loved ones are with us as long as we remember them. That is not what Jesus meant. His presence in and with the church is the source of the church's authority to discipline its members and the source of its power to evangelize the world.

Conclusion

The gospels are the earliest documents relating the life and teachings of Jesus. Those who aren't satisfied with portrait Jesus we find in the gospels try to reconstruct Him into a version more palatable to their anti-supernatural world views. Whether they see Him as a simple peasant preacher or a fiery, failed prophet of imminent doom, they must play fast and loose with the only source we have for the teachings of Jesus. They assume that Jesus must have said or not said certain things, based not on ancient manuscripts, but on their own preconceived notions of Him.

All I am maintaining is that gospels should be taken seriously. If you do that, you ought to conclude that Jesus taught –

➢ That He had a unique relationship with God the Father, a relationship that goes far beyond what He taught His disciples to claim.

➢ That He existed in glory with the Father before the foundation of the world; that He came down to earth from heaven; and that He was (or rather is) the great I AM.

➢ That His death and resurrection would be followed by His personal presence with His people, no matter where in the world they happened to go.

➢ That He would come again in glory with the holy angels to judge the world.

The career of the Christ as described in His own words is far different from what modern teachers of religion wish to believe about Him.

Chapter 11

The Father is Greater

Challenges to the deity of Christ come from many directions. In this chapter I will deal briefly a group of texts regularly utilized by Jehovah's Witnesses to lure unwary seekers into their cult.

The Trinity

The Jehovah's Witnesses classify as a cult because they deny biblical doctrines that are essential for salvation. These doctrines are taught in the classic creeds of the church, which are accepted by conservative Protestants, by Roman Catholics, and by the Orthodox family of churches.

Chief among these essential doctrines is the doctrine of the Trinity. All classic branches of the Christian church teach the doctrine of the Trinity. Although the word Trinity never appears in the Bible, it is a useful word to describe the Threeness and Oneness of God.

There is only one God who eternally exists as three distinct persons. If we said that three gods were one God, we would be contradicting ourselves. If we said that the three persons were one Person, we would be speaking nonsense. The doctrine of the Trinity says that Yahweh is One in one way and Three in a different way. Yahweh is one in His divine essence and three in His personhood. This is not contradictory.

The doctrine of the Trinity may be summarized in three short statements.

1) There is only one God.
2) There are three Persons who are God.
3) These three Persons are distinct.

The familiar Trinitarian triangle presents the same truths in a visual form.

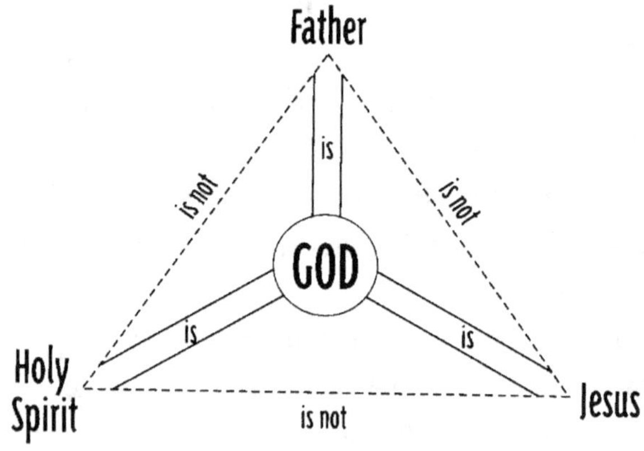

For a more thorough explanation of the Trinity, see my books: *The Beauty of God for a Broken World* (chapters 10-11) and *Practical Bible Doctrine* (Appendix C). My goal in this chapter is more limited. I will deal with some texts Jehovah's Witnesses use to attempt to prove that Jesus is not fully God.

Jesus Is Equal to the Father

We have already seen Jesus claiming a degree of honor equal to Father's honor (John 5:23). This is particularly significant given God's insistence that He will not share His glory with another (Isaiah 42:8; 48:11). Just to drive this nail home before we pass on to texts that seem to suggest otherwise, consider Revelation 5:11-14.

> Then I looked, and I heard the voice of many angels around the throne and the living creatures and the elders; and the number of them was myriads of myriads, and thousands of thousands, saying with a loud voice, "Worthy is the Lamb that was slain to receive power and riches and wisdom and might and honor and glory and blessing." And every created thing which is in heaven and on the earth and under the earth and on the sea, and all things in them, I heard saying, "To Him who sits on the throne, and to the Lamb, *be* blessing and honor and glory and dominion forever and ever." And the four living creatures kept saying, "Amen." And the elders fell down and worshiped.

Every degree of honor and glory and worship ascribed to God the Father is also ascribed to the Lamb, who is Jesus Christ. Yahweh is a jealous God who does not share His worship with another. Therefore, Jesus is Yahweh and is equal to God the Father.

Common Challenges

Jehovah's Witnesses commonly ask if Jesus is God, why did He pray to the Father? For example, in the garden of Gethsemane, Jesus said, "My Father, if it is possible, let this cup pass from Me; yet not as I will, but as You will" (Matthew 26:39).

The submission of Jesus in the face of the cross is simply the capstone of life-long submission. He said, "For I have come down from heaven, not to do My own will, but the will of Him who sent Me" (John 6:38). In fact, throughout His ministry Jesus only did and taught what the Father gave Him.

> Therefore Jesus answered and was saying to them, "Truly, truly, I say to you, the Son can do nothing of Himself, unless *it is* something He sees the Father doing; for whatever the Father does, these things the Son also does in like manner (John 5:19).

> So Jesus answered them and said, "My teaching is not Mine, but His who sent Me (John 7:16).

> So Jesus said, "When you lift up the Son of Man, then you will know that I am *He*, and I do nothing on My own initiative, but I speak these things as the Father taught Me (John 8:28).

Passages like these do not prove that Jesus was not God. Rather, they prove one of the key elements of trinitarian doctrine: The persons of the Godhead are distinct. Jesus is not just another name for the Father. Jesus is not the Father, and the Father is not Jesus. Because they are distinct persons, they relate to each other in ways that are appropriate to the roles they have assumed in creation, judgment, and redemption.

Putting It All Together

It is significant that the gospel in which Jesus makes His clearest claim to equality with the Father (John 5:23; 8:56-58) is also the gospel in which His submission to the Father is most frequently asserted. The apostle John apparently wanted us to hold tightly to both of these truths.

How do they fit together? How can the both be true? Philippians 2 draws both truths together into a glorious harmony.

> Have this attitude in yourselves which was also in Christ Jesus, who, although He existed in the form of God, did not regard equality with God a thing to be grasped, but emptied Himself, taking the form of a bond-servant, *and* being made in the likeness of men. Being found in appearance as a man, He humbled Himself by becoming obedient to the point of death, even death on a cross. For this reason also, God highly exalted Him, and bestowed on Him the name which is above every name, so that at the name of Jesus every knee will bow, of those who are in heaven and on earth and under the earth, and that every tongue will confess that Jesus Christ is Lord, to the glory of God the Father (verses 5-11).

Before the incarnation, Jesus existed in the form of God. He appeared as He really was. Through the incarnation He took on the form of a servant, becoming in fact what He had not been before, that is, the Servant of the Lord. Many assume that when Jesus emptied Himself, He lost some of His divine attributes, but that is not what the text says. He didn't empty Himself by losing something. He emptied Himself by adding something. When He took on the form of a servant, He deliberately hid His divine glory. He appeared to be an ordinary man just like the rest of us, but He was a sinless man and a man in whom all the fulness of the Godhead dwelt (Colossians 2:9).

As a man, the Son of God was able to be crucified. As a man, He was raised from the dead. As a man God highly exalted Him. Now there is a man in heaven to whom every knee shall bow. What is the name that God has bestowed on this exalted man? Consider the passage Paul that quotes in Philippians 2:10—Isaiah 45:22-23, where Yahweh says,

> Turn to Me and be saved, all the ends of the
>   earth;
> For I am God, and there is no other.
> I have sworn by Myself,
> The word has gone forth from My mouth in
>   righteousness
> And will not turn back,
> That to Me every knee will bow, every tongue will
>   swear *allegiance*.

In Philippians we read that every knee will bow to Jesus. In Isaiah Yahweh says that every knee will bow to Him. There is no other God besides Yahweh. Therefore, the name given to the man Jesus is Yahweh. That name is His by right because He was Yahweh before the incarnation. When Jesus ascended to the Father's right hand, the Father declared that this Man is Yahweh. Every sentient being in all creation will be compelled to acknowledge that fact and to bow before the sovereign majesty of Jesus.

Trinitarian Roles

The confession that Jesus is Lord (i.e. Yahweh) will redound "to the glory of God the Father" (Philippians 2:11). This phrase brings us back to the roles that the Father, Son, and Holy Spirit assumed for our redemption. In the gospel of John, the Holy Spirit glorifies Jesus (16:14) and Jesus glorifies the Father (17:1, 4). The same truth appears in Paul's triumphant chapter on the resurrection of Christ. Looking forward to the consummation of all things, the apostle writes, "When all things are subjected to Him [Christ], then the Son Himself also will be subjected to the One who subjected all things to Him, so that God may be all in all (1 Corinthians 15:28).

What shall we make of these things? Scripture clearly teaches that Jesus is equal in power, glory, and honor to the Father. It also teaches that the persons of the Godhead do different things in creation, redemption, and consummation. The Son was not forced to subject Himself to the Father, but He willingly took that place.

> Therefore, when He comes into the world, He says,
> "Sacrifice and offering You have not desired,
> But a body You have prepared for Me;
> In whole burnt offerings and *sacrifices* for sin You
> 	have taken no pleasure.
> Then I said, 'Behold, I have come
> (In the scroll of the book it is written of Me)

To do Your will, O God'"
(Hebrews 10:5-7, quoting from Psalm 40:6-8).

The Son came into the world for the specific purpose of doing God's will. That was His choice. That was His delight (Psalm 40:8) because He loves the Father (John 14:31).

The problem Jehovah's Witnesses have is that they accept the passages that teach the Son's submission to the Father, but they ignore the indications that this submission was voluntary, and they ignore the passages that teach His equality with the Father. The orthodox doctrine of the Trinity accepts both sets of passages.

The Father Is Greater

That brings me at last to the prime passage Jehovah's Witnesses love to quote. As He was preparing His disciples for His death, resurrection, and ascension into heaven, Jesus said, "You heard that I said to you, 'I go away, and I will come to you.' If you loved Me, you would have rejoiced because I go to the Father, for the Father is greater than I" (John 14:28).

In what sense is the Father greater than Jesus? The Father is not greater than the Son in their essential deity. He is greater in the outworking of the divine plan formed before the foundation of the world. Theologians sometimes call this plan the Covenant of Redemption. The name we use for this voluntary agreement among the persons of the Godhead is irrelevant, but there is clear Scriptural evidence for it.

God the Father chose a people in Christ before the foundation of the world (Ephesians 1:3-4). He gave these people to His Son for the Son to redeem (John 6:37-40). The Father sent the Son into the world, and the Son willingly went. The roles of Chooser/Sender and Sent One/Redeemer were not necessary nor were they arbitrary. It was suitable for the Father to choose and to send. It was suitable for the Son to be sent and to redeem. Because it was suitable, the Son said, "I delight to do Your will, O my God" (Psalm 40:8). Therefore, when Jesus said, "The Father is greater than I," He was referring to His voluntary role in the outworking of redemption, not to His essential deity.

A Few Loose Ends

I considered including a discussion of the inaccurate rendering of John 1:1 in the *New World Translation* produced by the Jehovah's Witnesses. The standard English translations of this verse say, "In the beginning was the Word, and the Word was with God, and the Word was God." The Jehovah's Witnesses' *New World Translation* renders the last clause, "and the Word was a god."

I read the Greek New Testament regularly, and I can say with great assurance that the *New World Translation* is wrong. However, I cannot explain why it is wrong without teaching you some of the finer points of Greek grammar. Even then, you would just be relying on my say-so.

Instead, I want to remind you of a clear affirmation of Christ's deity from His own lips that does not depend on any knowledge of Greek. When Jesus appeared to His disciples on the evening after His resurrection, Thomas was not present. When Jesus appeared again a week later, He invited Thomas to touch the nail prints in His hands and to thrust his hand into His side.

> Thomas answered and said to Him, "My Lord and my God!" Jesus said to him, "Because you have seen Me, have you believed? Blessed *are* they who did not see, and *yet* believed" (John 20:28-29).

On one occasion when I pointed this verse out to a Jehovah's Witness, he replied, "Well, Thomas wasn't calling Jesus his Lord and his God. He was shocked and those words just popped out. They were just an exclamation of surprise." However, if "my Lord and my God" was just an expression of amazement, Thomas was using the Lord's name in vain, and Jesus would not have commended him for his faith. The Lord would have condemned his irreverence, just as He is offended by the flippant use of "Oh my God" today. The third commandment says, "You shall not take the name of the LORD your God in vain, for the LORD will not leave him unpunished who takes His name in vain" (Exodus 20:7). Jesus clearly approved of Thomas's open confession of His deity.

The few loose ends category includes a couple of verses outside the gospels, that is, outside the scope of this study, so I'll be brief.

Revelation 2 and 3 consist of a series of letters from the risen Lord Jesus to seven churches in western Turkey. Each letter starts with an address followed by a description of Christ. The last of these letters begins, "To the angel of the church in Laodicea write: The Amen, the faithful and true Witness, the Beginning of the creation of God, says this" (Revelation 3:14). Jesus is the "Beginning of the creation of God" not because He was the first creature made by God (as Jehovah's Witnesses claim), but because He is source or origin of creation. "All things came into being through Him, and apart from Him nothing came into being that has come into being" (John 1:3).

Colossians 1:15 is another frequently misunderstood text: "He is the image of the invisible God, the firstborn of all creation." Firstborn does not mean first created, which would have been easy to express in Greek. The firstborn son in a Jewish family was the principal heir, and he became the head of the family upon his father's death. Jesus has the status of a firstborn because He is the heir of all things. These ideas come together in Hebrews 1.

> In these last days [God] has spoken to us in His Son, whom He appointed heir of all things, through whom also He made the world (v. 2).

> And when He again brings the firstborn into the world, He says, "And let all the angels of God worship Him" (v. 6).

The application of firstborn to Christ is based on Psalm 89 where the Lord says of David,

> I also shall make him *My* firstborn,
> The highest of the kings of the earth.
> My lovingkindness I will keep for him forever,
> And My covenant shall be confirmed to him
> (vv. 27-28).

Obviously, David was not God's firstborn son in any literal sense. He and his seed, culminating in Christ, have the title *firstborn*.

So, when Scripture calls Jesus the "firstborn of all creation," it simply means He is the heir of all creation because He is the Messiah, the ultimate son of David. Although Jesus is the heir, He is not a selfish older brother who keeps the inheritance for Himself. (See Luke 12:12 for an example.) Jesus shares the inheritance with us. We who have been adopted into the family of God are "fellow heirs with Christ" (Romans 8:17). What a privilege that is!

The denial of Christ's essential deity is not new with Jehovah's Witnesses. They are simply repeating the errors of a heretic named Arius (AD 256-336). These errors were condemned by the Council of Nicea in AD 325. The decision of this council is universally accepted as true to Scripture by all branches of the Christian church.

The words of Jesus Himself clearly indicate that He is equal in honor to the Father and that He submitted to the will of the Father because He loved Him. The New Testament epistles and Revelation elaborate on that equality and on the willing submission of the God-Man to the Father. Though we cannot know what it like for God to be God, our part is to praise the three in one.

> Praise the Father, praise the Son
> Praise the Spirit, three in one
> God of glory, Majesty
> Praise forever to the King of Kings
> ("King of Kings," Hillsong Music).

Chapter 12

Gnostic Distortions of Jesus

— ∽ —

Recent years have witnessed a resurgence of interest in Gnosticism, which was a second through fourth century fusion of Christianity with various external sources: (1) Greek philosophy, especially as re-interpreted by the Alexandrian Jew Philo; (2) Zoroastrianism (Persian religion); and (3) possibly some indirect influence from Buddhism.

In previous chapters of this book, I have focused on what Jesus said about Himself and how these statements ought to be viewed in the context the Old and New Testaments. The issue for this chapter is whether the Gnostic gospels provide us any new, reliable words of our Savior.

Modern opponents of orthodox Christianity have rallied around the notion that Gnosticism was a valid branch of Christianity that was ruthlessly suppressed by the victorious church. The scholars and popularizers who promote this interpretation of early Christianity have a clear agenda. It is to undermine the uniqueness and moral authority of orthodox Christianity. Consequently, they ignore the fact that Gnosticism doesn't have an historical leg to stand on, whereas biblical Christianity has two.

Christianity's two legs are the clear historical priority and accuracy of the New Testament documents over Gnostic writings, and the continuity of teaching from the apostles through the early leaders of the church. Before looking at these two firm foundations of historic Christianity, let's take a quick glance at the basic tenets of Gnosticism.

Gnostic Notions

Gnosticism was not an organized religion. It is represented by an amorphous collection of teachers and texts who shared some of the following ideas.

➤ Salvation comes not through faith, but through knowledge (the Greek word for knowledge is *gnosis*) that is available only to the few who have been initiated into it.

➤ Matter is evil; spirit is good.

➤ The physical world was created by a demiurge that was infinitely remote from the Supreme Being. The demiurge was identified with the God of the Old Testament.

➤ The humanity of Christ was not real. He only appeared to be human. The pure Christ-Spirit could not be joined to evil matter. Therefore, His sufferings on the cross were only apparent, not real.

➢ The separation of evil matter and pure spirit led different teachers to opposite conclusions. Some insisted on strict asceticism to keep the evil flesh under control. Others taught that since the flesh could not touch the pure spirit, those *in the know* were free to indulge the desires of the flesh as much as they pleased.

Full-blown Gnosticism did not develop until the second century AD. Even in first century, however, some proto-gnostic teachings had begun to invade the church. The apostle Paul combated strict asceticism in Colossians 2:20-23 and 1 Timothy 4:1-5. The falsely called "knowledge" that was leading many astray included "myths and endless genealogies" propagated by Jewish teachers (1 Timothy 1:3-7; 6:20-21; Titus 1:14).

The apostle John warned the church about false teachers who denied that Jesus had a real body of flesh (1 John 2:22; 4:1-3). He reminded his readers that true knowledge is not the right of the initiated few. All who believe in the Son of God may know that they have eternal life (2:20-21; 5:13).

Finally, by the end of the first century, some churches had been corrupted by "the teaching of Balaam" who encouraged God's people to "eat things sacrificed to idols and to commit *acts of* immorality" (Revelation 2:14-15, 20). This may be related to the gnostic notion that the pure spirit cannot be corrupted by the deeds of the flesh.

Historical Priority of the New Testament

Are there extra books with secret information about Jesus that should be received as the word of God? That is the implication of Bart Ehrman's collection of religious texts from the second and third centuries AD: *Lost Scriptures: Books that Did Not Make It into the New Testament.* Not all of these are Gnostic texts, but many of them are. Ehrman is a legitimate, well-credentialed scholar, but his bias against orthodox Christianity is evident. The title and subtitle of his book suggest that these texts had a valid claim to be included in the New Testament. That suggestion is simply false.

Ehrman is correct in saying that it took over three hundred years for the church to arrive at a universal consensus on the final twenty-seven books that make up our New Testament. However, the four gospels, Acts of the Apostles, and the letters of Paul circulated widely and early and received immediate recognition by the churches. Some of the shorter letters along with Hebrews and Revelation took longer to be acknowledged by the whole church as having apostolic authority. Every theological student in evangelical seminaries knows this.[±]

[±] See Michael J. Kruger for a widely praised discussion of the canon from an evangelical and reformed position.

In addition, a few works from early in the second century were highly regarded by the churches. Their teachings were essentially orthodox, but since they were not written by someone in the apostolic circle, they were not received as Scripture. Examples include *The Didache* (AD 100-120) and *The Letter of Barnabas* (circa AD 130).

While the New Testament documents were all written in the first century, the dates Ehrman suggests for the texts he includes are all in the second and third centuries. Not only that, but the various books in Ehrman's collection are dependent on the canonical gospels and Acts.

For example, Ehrman says about *The Gospel of the Ebionites,* "It is difficult to assign a date to this Gospel, but since it betrays a knowledge of Matthew, Mark, and Luke, and presupposes a thriving community of Jewish Christians, it is perhaps best to locate it sometime early in the second century" (Ehrman 13).

The gnostic Gospels do not provide a narrative of Jesus' ministry and the spread of the early church as the canonical gospels and Acts do. They assume that people are already familiar with the chief characters of these narratives—Peter, John, Mary Magdalene, and Paul. The celebrated *Gospel of Thomas,* for example, "records 114 'secret teachings' of Jesus. It includes no other material: no miracles, no passion narrative, no stories of any kind. What ultimately mattered for the author of Thomas was not Jesus' death and resurrection, which he does not narrate or discuss, but the mysterious teachings that he delivered" (Ehrman, 19).

The New Testament gospels and the Acts of the Apostles have clear historical priority over gnostic productions written decades or centuries later. Not only that, but the general historical reliability of the gospels and Acts has often been demonstrated. [±]

Continuity of Apostolic Teaching

Late in the second century, Irenaeus, the bishop of Lyons, France, responded to the claims of full-blown Gnosticism in a treatise called *Against Heresies* (Latin, *Adversus Haereses*). In books 1 and 2 of his treatise, Irenaeus describes the doctrines of leading Gnostic writers and answers them with theological and philosophical arguments. Book 3 introduces an important historical argument on the continuity of orthodox teaching.

The Gnostic teachers claimed that their doctrines had been secretly communicated by Jesus to His disciples. These secret teachings superseded the open teachings of Jesus recorded in Matthew, Mark, Luke, and John. Irenaeus responded,

> For if the apostles had known hidden mysteries, which they were in the habit of imparting to "the perfect" apart and privily from the rest, they would have delivered

---

[±] See F. F. Bruce for a classic defense of the New Testament's reliability. Though written by a world-renowned scholar, it is brief and highly readable.

them especially to those to whom they were also
committing the Churches themselves. For they were
desirous that these men should be very perfect and
blameless in all things, whom also they were leaving
behind as their successors, delivering up their own place
of government to these men (Irenaeus 3.3.1).

Irenaeus then notes that each of the churches
founded by an apostle was able to trace its leaders one
by one back to that apostle. These pastors, the successors
of the apostles, all taught the same truths that are
contained in the Scriptures. (Irenaeus specifically names
the four canonical gospels.)

"Since, however, it would be very tedious, in such a
volume as this, to reckon up the successions of all the
Churches," Irenaeus lists the twelve successors of Peter
and Paul, who were bishops at Rome (3. 3. 2-3). Even at
that early date, the church at Rome was highly regarded
by the other churches.

Irenaeus himself had met Polycarp, who "was not
only instructed by apostles, and conversed with many
who had seen Christ, but was also, by apostles in Asia,
appointed bishop of the Church in Smyrna" (3. 3. 4).
Neither Polycarp nor the successors of the apostles
taught any of the "secret" doctrines of the Gnostics.
Furthermore, the Gnostics could not trace their lineage
back to the apostles. Therefore, the Gnostic teachers had
no historical leg to stand on.

A Sampling of Gnostic Teachings

Perhaps the best refutation of Gnosticism is simply
to read some of their writings. The shocking difference

between them and the canonical gospels makes clear why the early church rejected them.

The Coptic Gospel of Thomas contains a number of sayings of Jesus that are similar to sayings in the gospels, but often with an unusual twist. It ends with this surprising interchange.

> Simon Peter said to them, "Let Mary leave us, for women are not worthy of life."
> Jesus said, "I myself shall lead her in order to make her male, so that she too may become a living spirit resembling you males. For every woman who will make herself male will enter the kingdom of heaven (Ehrman 28).

The Gospel of Peter describes the resurrection of Christ thus: The soldiers watching the tomb

> saw three men emerge from the tomb, two of them supporting the other, with a cross following behind them. The heads of the two reached up to the sky, but the head of the one they were leading went up above the skies. And they heard a voice from the skies, "Have your preached to those who are asleep?" And a reply came from the cross, "Yes" (Ehrman 33).

Needless to say, this is not a description of the physical body of the risen Christ that Thomas was allowed to touch.

The Infancy Gospel of Thomas (early second century) reports a number of miracles that Jesus supposedly did as a child. When he was five years old, "He then made some soft mud and fashioned twelve sparrows from it. It was the Sabbath when he did this" When Jesus was accused of profaning the Sabbath, he

"clapped his hands and cried to the sparrows, 'Be gone!'
And the sparrows took flight and went off, chirping"
(Ehrman, 58).

The same gospel recounts a more sinister miracle of
Jesus:

> Somewhat later he was going through the village, and a
> child ran up and banged into his shoulder. Jesus was
> aggravated and said to him, "you will go no further on
> your way." And right away the child fell down and died
> (Ehrman 58).

Does this sound like an authentic saying of Jesus Christ
as we hear Him in the gospels?

The Second Treatise of the Great Seth (third
century) denies that Jesus was crucified. Simon of
Cyrene, who bore Jesus' cross, was mistakenly taken for
Jesus and was crucified in His place. Christ describes the
crucifixion thus:

> For my death which they think happened, (happened) to
> them in their error and blindness. They nailed up their
> man up to their death. For their minds did not see me, for
> they were deaf and blind….
>
> Another, was the one on whom they put the crown of
> thorns. But I was rejoicing in the height over all the
> riches of the archons and the offspring of their error and
> their conceit, and I was laughing at their ignorance
> (Ehrman 84).

Can you imagine Jesus laughing at the poor scapegoat
who was crucified in His place?

The Secret Book of John (late second century)
recounts a revelation from Jesus to the apostle John after
Jesus had gone away. Jesus first declares that the Monad

is an invisible Spirit so high above all gods that he cannot be known, named, or described. From this Monad descended a series of lesser beings—gods or super-angels—called aeons. A number of these aeons are described. At the end of the list is Sophia (Wisdom) who created an aeon without the consent of her consort. This imperfect aeon created other lesser powers and the fallen, messed-up, material world where we live. Out of ignorance, this malformed aeon proclaimed himself the only god. He was the god of the Old Testament.

When human souls were trapped in mortal bodies, Christ came down to give them the knowledge they needed to escape. Christ describes the tree of knowledge of good and evil then he tells John, "But it was I who brought about that they ate."

John is understandably confused, "And I said to the savior, 'Lord, was it not the serpent that taught Adam to eat?'" The further explanation of the temptation is not easy to follow, but after a description of the creation of the first woman, Jesus continues,

> And our sister Sophia (is) she who came down in innocence in order to rectify her deficiency. Therefore she was called Life, which is the mother of the living, by the foreknowledge of the sovereignty of heaven.... And through her they have tasted the perfect Knowledge. I appeared in the form of an eagle on the tree of knowledge, which is the Epinoia from the foreknowledge of the pure light, that I might teach them and awaken them out of the depth of sleep.

The basic assertion of this passage is that it was good that our first parents ate from the tree of the knowledge of good and evil because salvation comes through knowledge.

Does this sound at all like the Jesus of the gospels? No! And that is what doomed second and third century Gnosticism to obscurity until it was more recently revived as a so-called authentic alternative to orthodox Christianity.

Scholars and popularizers who promote this view imply that the proto-orthodox church persecuted the poor Gnostics out of existence. The fact is that the church itself was persecuted during these centuries. It had no ability to persecute anybody until it finally gained the upper hand in the fourth century. By then Gnosticism was already on the wane. It had lost the battle for the hearts of the masses for several reasons.

First, church leaders like Irenaeus had successfully shown that Gnosticism did not have an historical leg to stand on. Second, unlike the Gnostics, the church did not hide its teaching behind a veil of secret knowledge. The preaching of the gospel was open to all. Third, Gnosticism had no power to transform lives, as the gospel did. Finally, Jesus in the canonical gospels spoke clearly and powerfully so that the crowds were amazed by his teaching. The Jesus of the Gnostic gospels spoke arcane mumbo-jumbo.

Those who want to hear Jesus in His own words need go no further than the New Testament. That is what God's people soon realized. That is the reason the church rejected Gnosticism.

Concluding Remarks

—⁓—

Although there are a few brief historical references to the existence of Jesus within a hundred years of His crucifixion,± we have no reliable records of His teaching outside of the canonical gospels. Scholars who try to get behind the gospels to discover a peasant preacher who never claimed to be divine are just flapping their arms in the air like an injured bird trying unsuccessfully to get off the ground.

On the other hand, extra-biblical sayings of Jesus in the Gnostic writings have no legitimate connection with the historical Jesus. Unlike the peasant preacher of critical scholars, the Gnostics portray Him as a kind of super-angel or benevolent Christ-Spirit who saves not through His death and resurrection but through arcane knowledge available only to the few.

When we look at the gospels to see what Jesus actually said, we find unmistakable claims to deity.

± By Josephus (Jewish historian, AD 37-100); Tacitus (Roman historian, AD 56-120); Pliny the Younger (Roman lawyer, AD 61-c.113).

➢ He claimed the kind of allegiance from His followers that supersedes all human ties. They must be willing to lose their very lives for His sake.

➢ He claimed to be greater than the prophets, greater than Solomon, greater than the temple, greater than the Sabbath, and worthy of honor equal to that of God the Father.

➢ He claimed to give rest to weary souls, living water to the spiritually thirsty, and eternal life to those who believe in Him. Those who reject Him will fall under His eternal judgment at the last day.

➢ He claimed to be the good Shepherd who seeks and finds His lost ones and who has a supernatural knowledge of His sheep.

➢ He claimed that He existed before His birth, that He come down from heaven, and that He would return again at the end of the age.

➢ He claimed that He was the Son of God, and praised Thomas for confessing that He was "my Lord and my God" (John 20:28).

On almost every page of the gospels, Jesus said things that would be outrageously blasphemous if He were not indeed God—not *a god*, but God Himself. Therefore, the issue for all human beings—for you—is this: Will you trust Him as your Savior and serve Him as your Lord and God?

Works Cited

— ❧ —

Augustine. *Confessions.*
https://en.wikisource.org/wiki/Nicene_and_Post-Ni
cene_Fathers:_Series_I/Volume_I/Confessions/Boo
k_I

Bruce, F. F. *The New Testament Documents: Are They Reliable?* Sixth Edition with a new forward by N. T. Wright. Published jointly by Wm. B. Eerdmans and InterVarsity Press, 1981.

Carson, D. A. *The Gospel according to John* in The Pillar New Testament Commentary. Grand Rapids: William B. Eerdmans, 1991.

Durant, Will. *Our Oriental Heritage, The Story of Civilization*, vol. 1. New York: Simon and Schuster, 1954.

Ehrman, Bart D. *Lost Scriptures: Books that Did Not Make It into the New Testament.* Oxford University Press, 2003.

Irenaeus. *Against Heresies.*
www.ccel.org/ccel/schaff/anf01.html.

Michael J. Kruger. *Canon Revisited: Establishing the Origins and Authority of the New Testament Books*. Wheaton: Crossway, 2012.

Lewis, C. S. *Mere Christianity*. New York: The MacMillan Company, 1958.

Keil, C. F.. *Minor Prophets* in *Commentary on the Old Testament*, vol. 10, by C. F. Keil and F. Delitzsch. Grand Rapids: William B. Eerdmans, reprint edition 1973.

About the Author

— ∾ —

Dr. John K. LaShell was a pastor for forty-seven years. He has a BA from Moody Bible Institute, an MA from Talbot Theological Seminary, and a PhD from Westminster Seminary. He has been married to Heather for over fifty years. They have two believing children and four grandchildren. He now resides in Boone, NC, where he and Heather are actively serving the Lord as volunteers in a local church. His previous books include:

The Beauty of God for a Broken World: Reflections on the Goodness of the God of the Bible (CLC Publications, 2010).

Limping Christians: Help for Those Who Hobble along the Path of Life (2014)

Practical Bible Doctrine: How to Live out What You Believe (2017)

Imaginary Ideas of Christ: A Scottish-American Debate (2017; my PhD dissertation, 1985)

The Earth-Two Adventures, 4 vols. (2015-2018). This is a series of fantasy adventures for children and early teens.

Further information is available at the author's website: www.godisbeautiful.com . The books are available from

Amazon.com or from the author. Feel free to write the author at jklashell@gmail.com or jklashell@godisbeautiful.com.

www.ingramcontent.com/pod-product-compliance
Lightning Source LLC
Chambersburg PA
CBHW072052150726